UP FROM THE ASHES, FINDING HOPE AND PURPOSE

How to Rise Up and Embrace Your Resilience

Tiffany Modica, PsyD

ISBN 979-8-89112-268-0 (Paperback)
ISBN 979-8-89112-284-0 (Hardcover)
ISBN 979-8-89112-269-7 (Digital)

Covenant Books
11661 Hwy 707
Murrells Inlet, SC 29576
www.covenantbooks.com

Dedicated to all those who have survived trauma and life's difficulties. I am grateful you are reading this: may you find hope, healing, and purpose in your story. I believe in you. May you rise up and embrace your resilience and share your story with others, making an impact.

Thank you to God for his amazing grace, love, and hand in my life, even when I was not fully aware of it. I am here because of his compassionate love.

Thank you for those that have been there in my life. I am grateful to you all from the bottom of my heart. This includes my dear friends, family, my adopted parents, and my precious children, who are emblems of God's love and grace in my life: thank you for believing in me, for your grace, strength, and support in my life. I would not be who I am today without your imprint.

Thank you to those who decided to stay a part of my life before and since my growth and healing. You mean a great deal to me.

To the first responders, medical professionals, therapists, mentors, teachers, professors, and various people like my foster mom Jean, whom God used during the tender years (and later) to impact my life: thank you (looking up to Heaven).

Thank you to Wayne and Diane for being faithful to God's calling to minister to foster children God's love and imbed resilience into your curriculum at Royal Family Kid's Camp. This camp set the stage for me to have seeds of resilience planted in my life, hope, and know the Lord personally. Thank you for encouraging me to write my story in a book for others since my twenties, when I first stood on a stage to share.

Thank you all, and those unnamed that God used as well. God sees you all. God bless you.

With gratitude and love~

BOOK REVIEWS

Dr. Modica's story is one of intense resiliency, hope, and faith. She beautifully weaves psychological concepts with her lived experiences and Christian worldview. Her work evidences the power of healing through faith, relationships, and believing in one's own internal power to overcome trauma. This book is going to help so many people! Tiffany, you are truly a miracle!

—Gina Atencio-Maclean, PsyD
Licensed Clinical Psychologist, San
Clemente Psychological Services

Tiffany shares her story of resilience and Hope in her beautiful memoir. For those of you who are searching for something more beyond just the day-to-day survival of life, please read this book! You won't regret it.

—Brook Benda, MS
Professor of Social Psychology,
Concordia University Irvine.

Phenomenal story! So many powerful moments in the book! God is doing work in and through you. Redemptive and purpose-filled.

—Joanne Feldmeth, MA
Lifelong advocate for abused and trau-
matized children, former Vice President
for Clubs and Mentors at Royal Family
Kids, Former Executive Director of Child
SHARE, author of *Child Sexual Abuse—
The Clinical Interview* (1988), and *We Weep
for Ourselves and Our Children: A Guide for
Survivors of Child Sexual Abuse* (1990)

At a time when our society is reporting record levels of anxiety and distress, sharing stories of hope and thriving becomes that much more essential. With this book, Dr. Modica humbly models the mindset needed to move forward in spite of past trauma, courageously and generously sharing insights gained on her own path from devastation to renewal, as well as her clinical experience. If you are traveling on the road of healing and recovery, I would encourage you to invite Tiffany and her story to accompany you on your journey.

—Bill Fiala, PhD
Licensed Clinical Psychologist,
Journeys Counseling Ministry

Although it is full of true horrors, Tiffany's story is actually about the amazing healing and redemption that she experienced and how a life of suffering can become a life marked by love and compassion.

—Samuel Girguis, PsyD
Licensed Psychologist, Dept Chair, and
Director of the Doctoral Program in Clinical
Psychology at Azusa Pacific University

We first met Tiffany at one of our Royal Family Kids' Camps (as a foster child). She was shy and happy to participate in the many new experiences the camp had to offer. We remember her being so impacted by the guest speaker as a soloist and how that gave her hope for her future in singing. To know her today is an unquestionable miracle of God's grace and healing in her life. We are so proud of her for all she has accomplished—including producing this book, a testament to God's faithfulness in her life.

—Diane and Wayne Tesche
Co-Founder & Vice President of Operations
& Training, Ret., Royal Family Kids, Inc.

Tiffany has a whimsical writing style. I really enjoyed hearing her voice. I loved the picture of the Golden Thread. I read it over and over, and with my favorite drink, Dr. Pepper, next to me. This is a great book for many clients to read. I love the focus on God. This thrills my heart! Good job!

—For the Children: Wayne Tesche,
Co-Founder of Royal Family Kids, Inc.

FOREWORD

Randy Powell, LMFT, Pastor, and Founder and Executive Director of Journeys Counseling Ministry

As you will find out as you read *Up from the Ashes, Finding Hope and Purpose*, Tiffany starts off her book with letters from her children. At the end of the book, she writes a letter to them. This is a reflection of the personal nature of this book and the power of healthy relationships. I would like to borrow from this process by writing a personal letter to Tiffany.

Open Letter to Tiffany:

I write this to you from the view of a father, pastor, psychotherapist, friend, boss, and coworker. As you know, in my series of books entitled *Vigilant to Vibrant, It's Not A Bear!* I discuss reacting to events as if we are facing a grizzly bear (living vigilantly) while, in fact, most of the time, we are only facing a teddy bear. About 70 percent of the time, we react to events in our lives as if we are facing grizzlies. In reality, we are only facing grizzly bear situations about 5 to 6 percent of the time. We live in an escalated (vigilant) state of mind for most of our lives, missing out on seeing the blessings in life that lead to vibrant living. But in your book, you tell the story of facing constant grizzly bear situations and finding the way to vibrancy.

I am humbled and honored to write this Foreword. You are courageous, not only during your childhood but even in the now of your life!

You are an encouragement and model for us all. I have only respect and awe for you and not pity! You are no victim but a "warrior," and even more, you are a "warrior model" for all of us! Although I have not experienced the level of trauma you have been through, my trauma is mine, and I am encouraged to face my trauma intuitively with honesty and vulnerability and become a warrior. You have shown us resilience is accessible if we are willing to stand up and fight, be responsible for our lives, and be diligent.

It is a privilege and blessing to have you as a part of our journeys. I am committed to helping you reach out to all traumatized people of the world (all of us) and give us hope, direction, and courage to become warriors. Like a great painting by a great master of old, we are Masterpieces. We need to grasp that reality no matter how much marring, scarring, and painting we have done to ourselves or how much others have done to us. We fight like warriors so that NO ONE CAN DESTROY THE MASTERPIECE THE GREAT MASTER HAS MADE US TO BE! We are always masterpieces of the Creator, and he is still around to restore us to the glory he ordained us to be, no matter how "damaged" we have become by the evil of this world.

You are a beautiful masterpiece bringing a reflection of the Master to the world through your heart, mind, actions, and by just being Tiffany—his daughter!

You write with vulnerability, encouraging us to look at our whole being and see the real value—no matter the damage we have experienced to our bodies, minds, and emotions. You have made it clear that I am a masterpiece made by God—the Master of the universe. I am damaged (as we all are), scarred, and painted on, but I have the opportunity to be restored and find my purpose. You, by your life examples, give me the courage to be a warrior and find the purpose God has for me and see how beautifully I have been made.

As I followed your journey, I cried, felt sad, found joy, was impressed with you, was angry at what happened to you, was happy for your victories, and found the warrior inside of myself. You gave practical ways to heal and ways to identify and embrace my warrior-self as I read and interacted with the book.

Tiffany, I have never experienced the traumas you share, and yet I have experienced traumas throughout my life. The way you tell your story of traumas and grizzly bears allows me to see my own traumas with grace, hope, love, purpose, and a plan. No blame! No shame! No comparisons! No excuses! You are a warrior, and you inspire me to be a warrior as I face my own unique demons.

As I read your story, I could identify my own hurts, traumas, fears, lack of trust in others, betrayals, self-blame, survivor's guilt, desire to belong, and feeling of having no safe place. I did not have the severity of your experiences (though many reading this will have had horrible experiences similar to yours), but the hope and healing you have expressed are available to me and to all of us. You have shown me how not to be caught in the mentality of a victim—being held hostage by the horrible experiences that can come our way in this world. I can be a warrior—facing the issues with vulnerability leading to rewiring of my brain, having moments of celebrating God's love and presence in my life, and finding that a family is available to all of God's children.

Your accepting tenderness and caring heart come through the pages, which gives all of us the courage and strength to read the next page and move forward in our own story. Your definition of courage has challenged me to live a life of truth and vulnerability, leading to a vibrant Life.

I am proud of you and honored to be a part of your story. May anyone reading this book experience you as I have had the honor to over these years. How you express yourself in this book is exactly who you are in life. You are intelligent, loving, strong, encouraging, passionate, loyal, faith filled, grace filled, hopeful, resilient, a warrior, fierce in your zest for life, in other words, a powerful representative of the Creator!

LETTERS FROM MY KIDS

Dear Mom,

Even though you've gone through so much in your life, you're such a strong person that anyone can rely on. I know that it was really hard, but you've overcome so much, and I'm a proud son—I love you!

Love,
Jeremy (seventeen years old)

Dear Mom,

Though you went through something so hard, you used your experiences to help others overcome their own trauma. You working through your trauma and experience has also helped me work through my own. I've never met someone as strong and resilient as you. You are truly a blessing to be not only in my life, but my mother. I love you.

Love,
Rachel (fourteen years old)

CONTENTS

CHAPTER 1

I've Been There Too
Journeying through Foster Care and Trauma

If you are still breathing as you read these
words, your story isn't over.

—Greg Laurie
Author of *World Changers: How God Uses Ordinary
People to Do Extraordinary Things.*[1]

Welcome to the beginning of a journey, a bridge to a new adventure, a quest for truth, and a respite for peace. You are created for a purpose, and I am grateful you are here reading this. As you find yourself flipping through these pages, I want to illuminate your understanding. Each theme, story, message, and effort has been planted, one seed at a time, throughout my life to create a memoir of how I have survived and to provide you with something tangible to witness *real Hope.* I urge you to grab your beverage of choice, maybe a savory snack, a pencil or pen, and take time journeying with me through these stories, one at a time. I have survived many things, and so have you. Though our journeys may be different, they are alike in more ways than you may realize. I want to begin by telling you that you are strong and courageous, and though life may have weathered you,

---

[1] Greg Laurie, *World Changers: How God Uses Extraordinary People to Do Extraordinary Things* (Michigan: Baker Books, 2020), 20

you are here for a purpose and are so valued. I invite you to join me, arm-in-arm, as I unveil a life of surviving trauma and coming up from the ashes. As you journey alongside me, some things may come up. I encourage you to take time to care for yourself. Curl up in a blanket with a comforting cup of tea, find a friend to hug, or take a break walking outside. This journey requires an open heart, a willingness to grow, courage with perseverance, and self-care when needed. Remember, you and your story are so vitally important.

Have you ever found yourself feeling alone, feeling shame, having terrible memories come flooding back, wondering if you will ever survive or if the pain will ever stop? Have you found yourself in a place of utter disbelief, loss beyond words, wanting so badly to feel like you belong and matter and not feel invisible anymore? I've been there too. My hope is you may know you are not alone, and there is hope, but the journey can be arduous. The storms of life can feel overwhelming, so daunting that you want to run away and even feel hopeless at times. But, if there is one thing I want you to know, it is that "you are here for a reason." The fact that you are alive and reading this now means you are here for a purpose. You have breath in your lungs, and your heart is beating—you are alive and have much to offer. Hang on because we will journey on a roller coaster called life. As you read these words, remember I am right here beside you. Whatever your faith and perspective are, it is evident that you are created with intention, and "…everything…finds its purpose in Him (God)" (Colossians 1:16, MSG)[2]. Even Job, a man who struggled with challenges and remained steadfast in his faith in God in the Old Testament of the Bible, experienced a great deal of loss, and God redeemed his story. He had to struggle through tremendous grief and discover God's purpose in the midst of pain and suffering, even when his friends had doubts. I have encountered several hills, valleys, and treacherous storms, but I am here to tell my tale. For now, here is the beginning of my journey as a young child, having no compass and no guidance.

---

[2]   Colossians 1:16 (Message)

Growing up on the streets, particularly in a desert-laden small town, I did not know anything different. I would go from place to place, noting when the sun would come up, when it was another day, and when the night would come, then it was another night. I was never allowed near the windows, so I would watch the light peer through the drapes or outdoors to determine when it was day. I learned to *observe* time, people, and situations around me to help me through the day, and moment by moment, through experiences of survival and fear. However, sometimes, my mom would buy McDonalds. I knew this because I would see the yellow "M" sign illuminated at the driveway entrance. Most of the time, I never noticed I was hungry because I became so used to not eating. I had never actually been physically alone, being with my mom, but *I always felt alone.* I had no toys, only one pair of clothes, no shoes, and no one to play with. I never went to school or did doctors brush my teeth. I did not grow up with a parent tending to my wounds or reflecting on myself or the meaning of life. *I truly felt alone.* Occasionally, we would go to a store, and I would see Barbie dolls and clothes and *wonder* what it would be like to dress her up and do her hair. Sometimes we would stay at motels, and if there was a pool, I would wear a long T-shirt and swim. How did I know how to swim? I never took formal lessons, nor did I have a mom who held me and taught me to float. I learned because I *taught* myself. When I was two years old, my mother would often hear voices, became emotionally upset talking to the voices, pacing back and forth rapidly, and talking to herself. She was so mad at me once that she locked me in a closet underneath the stairs for a whole day and whole night. I felt safer in the closet. One day, I sneaked out the front door and walked to the pool. I was very young, and most parents at this juncture would be petrified that their toddler was unattended near water, but I was *free!*

I loved being outdoors and enjoyed the water immensely, though moments like these were few. I was determined to *learn* how to *navigate* the waters. I felt peace and excitement at the thought of it, and even in dipping my tiny toes in the water. I would walk into the water and test it out. Could I float? I started to go down, even in the shallow end. Then I would *wonder*: Could I reach the bottom?

My legs were too short. Could I kick my legs really fast and stay in one place? I practiced these little *experiments* to see what I could do. *I never thought about what I couldn't do* at this age. I was *determined.* Eventually, I *discovered* that I had to *build strength,* so I began sitting on the steps, straightening my legs, pointing my toes, and kicking as hard as I could. Soon my legs became stronger. Then I would venture to the side of the pool, curl my fingers around the concrete, and shuffle my body around the edge of the water until I made it all the way around. I was proud of myself. Then, I would practice holding my breath underwater while being stationary and holding my breath, and eventually would kick and swim across the entire pool while holding my breath! At this point, even at two years old, I had accomplished my goal: to be outside, play, be free near the water, and survive. I often would have these little gut feelings about things. (I will share more about that later.) But little did I know that everything I learned would be used later in my life, even through adulthood. *Seeds of resilience* peppered into my life as I was *determined, observant of my environment, lived in wonder and curiosity, and believed something greater than I had to exist, that it was better than what I lived in. I just didn't know what.*

Moment of reflection

Can you recall your earliest memory where you saw yourself in a new way, tapped into your imagination, and felt a sense of strength or courage? No matter how small or big, I invite you to write about it. This is key in your journey to discover the beginning of your development of resilience. Even if you are unsure, I encourage you to let the creativity flow, and be open.

What I learned and put together happened over thirty-five years later; my life, purpose, and meaning came together in pieces, not all at once. When I was a toddler, I was literally in the moment, but it wasn't all glamorous; there were no beauty pageants, no awards, and no running around the backyard being silly. In fact, I lived alone with my biological mother, who had paranoid schizophrenia. Her initial emotional issues that surfaced around age twenty-nine changed her significantly after I was born. Due to mental health challenges, she had no capacity for empathy and lacked the skills to care for her basic hygiene and needs; therefore, she could not care for my needs. Essentially, I experienced a lack of mirroring, attunement, safety, and love from her—I grew up in my early fundamental years with no tender loving care (TLC). What this translates to is I raised myself as a young child. Even when she was not hearing voices or seeing things that were not there, she was focused on herself. She was a prostitute, and I was domestically human trafficked. Every childhood moment, from two years old to seven and a half years old, I was learning how just to make it through the day and survive in a culture that provided no warmth, comfort, or safety but rather used me. "How am I supposed to act? What do I do here? How do I survive there? Will I ever be free?" I was constantly battling between extremes of being physically harmed and tortured at night, sexually abused, malnourished, neglected, or trying to survive my biological mother's episodes when she was hallucinating about "the enemy" coming after her. I was constantly in a frying pan and then put back into the fire. Living in the ashes was normal for me. I learned to please others to survive, to be a chameleon, and to blend in with the environment, but I also learned to read others so as not to trigger them into hurting me more. These lessons, however, were not meant for a young, innocent child to take on; they were survival methods ingrained in the wiring of my brain. I constantly learned how to battle double and triple binds—situations where I would potentially die or be severely abused to the point of being utterly helpless, being left physically, emotionally, and psychologically wounded. Little did I know I was becoming a *warrior*—but for what purpose?

I had met *real warriors* in my life—those that served our country in the military and fought for our freedom, others who were heroes—who ran in front of a car to save a child, a firefighter that ran into a burning building to save animals, first responders who show up during mass shootings or natural disasters—those are the *real* warriors, right? As I grew in my capacity and understanding of human beings, I have met several individuals that have been "warriors:" fought and survived cancer, heartache, alcoholism, poverty, death of a child, divorce, addiction, abandonment, car accidents, abuse, job loss, infidelity, bullying, assault, human trafficking, exploitation, torture, job loss, bankruptcy, and even the murder of a loved one. These are real people that grew up in real-life difficulties, inconsequential to themselves, and suddenly encountered layers of escalating challenges. Who are these *warriors*? What makes them different from others?

Moment of reflection

Can you recall warriors, heroes, and individuals you've looked up to in your life since your early childhood years? Who are these people? What traits stood out that sparked your interest or passion in what they have done?

As I personally reflect, the truth is I felt that I was nothing special, had no special gifts, and certainly did not intervene on anyone's behalf. I felt purposeless as a little girl. I was placed in a terribly unfortunate situation, and no one even tried to help rescue me. I felt like I had no value. However, years later, as I sat with these remarkable men, women, children, teenagers, and older adults, I realized we all share something in common: *We have a piece inside us that needs to be seen and heard, to be validated, and appreciated, and we all need to be known, and know in our heart, soul, and mind that we matter.* We need someone to believe in us to feel loved and valued. If we've ventured into facing these traumas and truths and sitting with others in their realizations and realities, then maybe we are becoming what we are intended to become a *warrior.*

Moment of reflection

In reading these statements that there is something inside us of value, what do you see in yourself that is valuable, or you feel has never been identified as valuable? As you learn to reflect and see parts of yourself, I encourage you to be kind to yourself. Remember, I did not realize my value until much later in my journey, and the truth is, it is a process of identifying, voicing, and embracing your value daily.

In retrospect, I lived through many seasons in my life and encountered every trauma and loss fathomable. I felt lost at times and had no idea who I was except for the circumstances I encountered. I had trouble separating the circumstances as *not* defining who I really was. As a young, impressionable child, I encountered unimaginable things. I was drugged and severely abused physically, sexually, emotionally, and psychologically. I was objectified and cast aside. I dealt with that horror from birth to seven and a half years of age. As a child, that was *normal* for me. Then, later I went through foster care for five and half years, moving through several temporary placements. I was displaced and threatened, fighting for my life, meanwhile trying to acclimate socially and academically at school. I desperately was trying to make sense of why I had survived when others had not, holding onto survivor guilt and trying to process all that had happened to me during my prime developmental years. Part of me had pushed the memories of the trauma away subconsciously and only believed that the severe abuse had happened to my biological mother and that *she* was the one abused by all the men, not me. However, deep down, I knew the truth—I was never wanted by her; I was just used as bait for the men in the human trafficking ring. These stark realizations paralyzed me as they came in waves and as the trauma overwhelmed me and rocked my sense of safety and security. In addition to the trauma, I had not been socialized properly or experienced school and learning in a typical manner. Once I was in foster care, I had finally experienced one month of first grade, and by second grade, I did not know how to read, write, or do math. I felt stupid, invisible, and unwanted. I struggled, feeling like I did not fit in, and I often felt confused. I remember thinking when I was seven and a half years old that even though God had scooped me out of the terror from my earlier childhood, I still felt lost and had no permanent home. I did not belong, and I had no medical or dental care and no compass.

In foster care, I found myself presented to families like a dressed-up figure in a magazine, waiting for someone to admire me and desire to take me in as part of their family. I felt like an object again and had no place where I belonged. Meanwhile, I was still trying to make sense of the family that had abandoned me. I so longed to have an anchor for my soul and a place to call home where I would be loved and feel safe. At the same time, I often wondered, what was the point of being rescued by the police? Which was worse? These double binds left me feeling overwhelmed, alone, and paralyzed.

Later in my life, I experienced a first adoption failure, betrayal in adult relationships, felt missed and overlooked often, and a lack of nurturance, attunement, and understanding that I needed to navigate the PTSD and nightmares I encountered. The effects of my early childhood impacted aspects of my adulthood too. I longed to be free. I felt trapped in a body that was reliving every piece of memory from my childhood, trying to resolve it, and I had to act "normal" like everyone else because there was very little understanding about the developmental, biological, emotional, social, and psychological impact of trauma. *I knew on some level that none of it was my fault* that I was not like my biological mother. However, I felt this sense of responsibility because no one stepped in to protect me or tell me I was valued and loved, and I never *felt* loved. At times, a tidal wave of memories would hit me, and I felt like I was imparted with an enormous responsibility to patch everything up and "pretend" like nothing happened, move on with my life, not even knowing what I was moving on from, or to, in my life.

Moment of reflection

Have you ever felt like you were not good enough or that it was not okay to just be who you authentically are, whether due to the pressure of others or yourself? Or have you ever just wanted to escape and pretend like nothing happened, just to give yourself some oxygen?

As I journeyed through complex trauma and layers of difficulties, I often felt like I was wandering. I did not really know who I was or my value. Instead, I began to practice reading others and pleasing them to survive. After all, as a little girl, I had been trained to turn tricks and handle double binds. I learned how to navigate survival like a pro.

Moment of reflection

Have you ever felt the need to accommodate others, make them happy, or do so to survive? Have you ever felt like the bane of your existence was for others, and you were just simply "used" by others? Valueless, purposeless, with no beauty, only ashes of pain, despair, and disgust, and not even having an inkling of what love and acceptance or sacrifice meant?

I remember growing up thinking, "No one understands me, and I am too much for them." However, I tried not to be a "problem child" but became like a chameleon, not knowing who I could trust. I had decided I would never take drugs or become an alcoholic, or go into prostitution because I grew up around it and saw the terrorizing effects it had on me from adults. I did not want to become the monsters that I had to submit to in my earlier childhood. As I grew up and met others with struggles with alcoholism and drugs, I empathized with their pain because I felt it too. However, instead of self-medicating, I would self-blame because, after all, no one took responsibility, so *I must be the problem*. I lived in deep shame but not depression. I had a past therapist estimate that she thought I lived in such long-term grief from the innocence taken and terror encountered, with extreme isolation and neglect while living under the hands of extremely sick individuals with severe issues who chose to act in inhumane and evil ways, that I was living in a state of melancholy and deep sadness from the loss of safety and well-being that was utterly deficient. I lived with intense anxiety and fear of being harmed, I would have recurring nightmares, and I experienced severe fears of interactions with certain types of people—particularly narcissistic, domineering, punishing, and critical types. I constantly lived in survival mode, not knowing if I would be taken away, abused, fed, or used as bait for men again. My fears were real. I was living a nightmare.

These memories brought me to my knees often. Throughout my life, I have found comfort in music and singing. As I reflect on Avril Lavigne's lyrics to "Nobody's Home,"[3] this piece encapsulates my childhood and adulthood:

> I couldn't tell you,
> Why she felt that way,
> She felt it every day.
> I couldn't help her,
> I just watched her make the same mistakes again.
> What's wrong, what's wrong now?
> Too many, too many problems
> Don't know where she belongs,
> Where she belongs
> She wants to go home,
> But nobody's home.
> That's where she lies
> Broken inside.
> With no place to go,
> No place to go,
> To dry her eyes,
> Broken inside.
> Open your eyes,
> And look outside,
> Find a reasons why.
> You've been rejected,
> And now you can't find,
> What you've left behind.
> Be strong, be strong now,
> Too many, too many problems.
> Don't know where she belongs;
> Where she belongs.
> She wants to go home,
> But nobody's home.

---

[3] Avril Lavigne, "Nobody's Home." Genius.com. June 1, 2023

It's where she lies
Broken inside.
With no place to go,
No place to go
To dry her eyes,
Broken inside.
Her feeling she hides,
Her dreams she can't find.
She's losing her mind.
She's fallen behind.
She can't find her place.
She's losing her faith.
She's fallen from grace,
She's all over the place.
She wants to go home,
But nobody's home.
It's where she lies
Broken inside.
With no place to go,
No place to go,
To dry her eyes,
Broken inside
She's lost inside, lost inside, ohh ohhh.[4]

I had an insatiable, deep longing to belong, experience love, feel safe, and have a home. The reality was I had none of these: No place to run to and cry or find solace from the aching, ongoing memories of terror that stole my childhood. I did not belong and would often experience waves of intense sadness and grief, that although it has not been my fault, I was forced to live through all this, but no one will ever see me for who I really am, except for the trauma that I survived. I would sometimes battle myself in thinking: *Oh, why did I survive, why?* I felt lost and meaningless at times. The tears would flood me. Being in foster care only solidified my belief that I was unwanted and did not

---

4   Avril Lavigne, "Nobody's Home." Genius.com. June 1, 2023.

belong. I was "bought," I was told, or I was not included with others, or chosen last, even cast aside or treated differently, and I was just "different" with no real family cultural traditions. Foster care is often thought of as a "third culture," but even then, I felt like I had no roots, no belonging, and no meaning. I often found comfort in comforting others because, after all, there must be some purpose in helping others. However, my heart longed to hear, "I really do understand because I lived through that, and I care. I see you, and you *are valuable!*" I dissociated much of this pain until later, meaning I had temporarily put it out of my present mind for years as a way to protect myself, and eventually had to do the brave work of processing the trauma and grief and learn to practice self-compassion and kindness toward myself.

Moment of reflection

Can you recall a time in your life when you felt invisible, felt used confused about your purpose, but even though others did not see you, you saw yourself? Something about you jumped out, like, Wait! This is important; I needed this, or do I believe in others who? What was that like? Despite how neglected I was growing up, I so longed to see others and support them in feeling loved, just as I needed to be seen, loved, and accepted. *Can you think of a song, a quote from a book, or a movie that resonated with something you struggled with in your life? Those moments of confirmation are growth moments. Hold onto them.* I've been there, too—you have experienced your own journey of difficulties, bumps, hurdles, or hurricanes. You are not alone, and yet, here you are. You have survived. But you are MORE than your trauma or life experiences. You are valuable, you have a purpose, and you have something special to offer the world. Healing is within reach. These chapters have passed for me, and many may have passed for you, but that does not mean your whole story is written. *You can rise up from the ashes and find hope and purpose. We can piece this together, one moment and a chapter at a time. I invite you to journal and reflect in between sections and chapters as you feel led. I invite you to join me in the next chapter of discovering hope in the midst of past pain.*

CHAPTER 2

Birthplace of Hope

We shall overcome because the arc of the moral
universe is long but bends towards justice.
—*Dr. Martin Luther King Jr*[5]

What do you recall as your favorite childhood adventures and memories? For me, growing up exploring nature, loving animals, attending birthday parties, doing sports, singing, dancing, and playing is expected of a normal childhood. This, however, was not my reality in my earlier childhood. I would contemplate my life on a deeper level, how to escape danger, how to read people, or wonder if there would ever be justice and resolution for the darkness surrounding me.

As a young, vibrant seven-year-old, I longed for a life different than the one I had, dressing up for fun, climbing trees, swimming in the pool, or playing with friends. However, I would shut down and push away those imaginative thoughts. One day I peered out the window and saw the blue sky and the sun beating on the earth and thought, "There *must be* something bigger than me that can rescue me from this situation." I was seven years old, living in Arizona, in the middle of being human trafficked, and felt imprisoned in the darkest evil imaginable. However, a glimmer of hope was in my eye,

---

5   Dr. Martin Luther King Jr. "Dr. Martin Luther King Jr." Smithsonian Institute. June 1, 2023. https://www.si.edu/spotlight/mlk?page=4&iframe=true.

and I had no idea where it came from. I quickly skirted to the side of the bed and pretended that I had not seen "the outside." I had to hide—that was the only way I could survive. I would look forward to moments, really any moment, to dip my toe in the water, see the blue sky, and just be a kid, but these moments were beyond rare.

One afternoon, around age six, my mother was more agitated and preoccupied than usual. I had been examining my surroundings, like when we were in a vehicle, looking at the buildings and sights around me. I would often look to see where the closest store was located or where the exit was. Today I was determined to be *free*. I calculated that my mother was in the bathroom and was not going to leave for some time. I crawled on the floor to the hotel door, quietly slid the chain lock off, and opened the door. I closed the door behind me ever so quietly as I held my breath. I knew we were on the second floor, and I attempted to crawl under the window, away from eyes catching me, to freedom. Just then, the door flew open, and faster than I could blink, she grabbed me under my arms and held me over the second-story balcony. My own flesh and blood mother told me if I ever tried this again, she would drop me. I froze in fear. Below was a glistening pool with concrete under me. I was terrified. She threw me into the hotel room and did unimaginable abuse to me because I sought freedom. When we lived out of state, I would survey the landscape and try to mastermind methods of escape from the head male perpetrator's apartment, again on a second story. I had imagined that if I broke the upstairs window, maybe I could land on the cars below and still be able to walk away, but it was too risky and, frankly, too loud. One day, I had planned when he was in his room with my biological mother, being abusive to her, I would open the door, go down the pebbled stairs, and run as fast as the wind to the 7-Eleven store on the corner and ask for help. I had planned it out and thought about it over and over, rehearsing it in my mind. However, it was too risky. Her "boyfriend," as she called him, was very tall, strong, and worked in an ambulance. He was very smart and knew how to manipulate people. One night, I defended my mother because I knew she was very "sick" and saw and heard things that weren't real. He took advantage of her. Then he took it out on me. I grew to have severe nightmares about this monster as he drugged me, forced me to drink beer, and hurt and abused me beyond comprehension. One time, I woke up in a black trash bag in the back of a car. I could peer out of a hole in the bag, and all I could think was, "How am I alive?" I was absolutely terrorized by this psychopath, and he did it at least two other times. Another memory I have is when my mom became pregnant. One day, she lost the baby, and I was confused as a young child, thinking she murdered it, finding the remnants in a trash can. I cried deeply. If this child had survived, I would *not* have been alone! But then again, this child could *never have survived here with no love, no food, and no one to care for her.* I cried, thought long and hard, and wondered, how am I surviving? I began to feel guilty about being alive. My mother would often pace and talk feverishly to herself in scary voices, often feeling paranoid that the enemy would come after her. One night, she was so enraged she was giving me a bath and threatening me that if I did not let her do things to me, she would drown me. I remembered it clearly that if I let her push me under the water of the bathtub, I would survive. So, I did. I held my breath. She pushed me under for a long time. I was grateful that I had taught myself how to swim and hold my breath. She had tried to drown me more than once. Then, she lifted me out of the water and abused me. Despite the double bind I was in, I had *survived*! I constantly had to read others, figure out how to survive, and choose the better of the two evils. My innocence was taken by her and several men multiple times in my earlier childhood. I wondered why I was still alive. She barely fed me, but a few times a week. *How* did I survive this long? I had never seen a doctor or a dentist or been to school. I wondered, how do I understand that I am nothing like her or the men? How do I believe there is something greater than me that can rescue me? Also, how am I able to wrestle with the phenomenological meaning of life and purpose when I was at the tender age of six and seven? These thought processes, I learned, were protective factors that helped sustain me when my earlier life was chaotic and made no sense.

So you are wondering, where is this "birthplace of Hope?" In the midst of such evil, there were glimpses of hope which began to peer into my life, like the touch of light I saw through the black trash bag, the moments when I held my breath and talked myself through it, the moment when I peered out the window reaching out to whatever was out there to come and save me. I began to develop this *strong belief* that I had survived and, therefore, there must be a *purpose in my life*. I decided at age seven, while living on the streets in Arizona and Southern California, that I was going to learn as much as I possibly could about the monsters that had harmed me for self-protection, and then I would seek out whatever it is that I was sensing has the capacity to create me the way I am, and see how it provides hope and way to escape the evil. I was *determined.*

Moment of reflection

Can you think of a time when you surprised yourself? You recognized an inner strength or understanding that you had not seen before? What was it like? Can you think of a time when you endured something really difficult and still saw light shining in the darkness? These are birthplaces of Hope. Mark these moments and remember them. They are key to linking with your resilience capacity.

Today's generation, in the twenty-first Century, calls these growth moments of strength *Grit* or *Resilience.* We all have the capacity to tap into this and develop it, but we need just enough internal strength and external resources to foster this development and use it effectively to flourish. Grit evokes the idea of gritting your teeth together, which involves intentionally digging your heels in, connecting with your internal strength, and courageously seeking out a way to master a situation. Resilience is similar, but it is like a ball that you drop and watch it bounce back. It is the capacity to engage with your whole self emotionally, physically, cognitively (in your mind and thinking), spiritually, and psychologically, and keep going despite difficulties. Both grit and resilience involve the ability to integrate your internal and external resources to problem-solve a situation and move through it, no matter the hurricane (or trauma) transpiring around it.

As a child, without fully knowing it, I was exercising my innate ability to reason with highly adult situations with the intent to *survive*. As I grew up and into adulthood, I needed to carry this toolbox and resource more tools, plus a village of support to unpack the immense complexity of trauma and find peace, hope, and redemptive healing. To do this, I needed to connect with my authentic self, trust my intuition, and with determination, move forward, believing good was around the corner.

A scary and miraculous experience occurred when my mom and I made our way from Arizona back to Southern California. My biological mom tried to check us into a motel, but something happened. Something triggered her to become very upset and all over the place mentally and emotionally. I was hidden in a vehicle, as I was not allowed to be out in public. The police came and arrested her. I witnessed it with my tender seven-year-old eyes. In shock and confusion, I yelled out, thinking they were hurting her. They were surprised that a child was in the car. They drove us separately to the Anaheim Police Department. There I witnessed my biological mother in handcuffs through glass windows, and with sadness and fear, I expressed, "She thinks you are hurting her! She needs help. I can help her! Stop!" The police sat me down and asked if I was five years old. I said, "Uh, No! I am seven and a half!" They were bewildered. It was evident I was extremely malnourished. They provided me with two peanut butter and jelly sandwiches and two glasses of milk, and I ate it in seconds—still hungry. They asked me several questions: Did anyone hurt you physically? Do you feel safe? The list went on. I refused to answer any questions. My job was to protect my biological mother. I later realized that I was experiencing Stockholm Syndrome and was wired to protect the only caregiver I knew, that also was my source of harm. Next, I was taken to Orangewood Children's Home, where I became a ward of the state and became a foster child. My biological mother came to visit me once and threatened my life and said that she would come after me if I told anyone. Then she left, and I was all alone. She took off, and the authorities told me that "she ran away from the police." My child instinct said to myself, "That made no sense. No one can get away from the police." I did not hear from her for years. After a few lonely placements in emergency shelter homes, I ended up at my main foster home. No one knew where to put me—I was too old for kindergarten but had no schooling. I started school for the first time in first grade in June and barely finished one month before school ended. I was so lost and confused, but I started to feel a sense of safety with my foster mom Jean. My life was beginning to unfold for the first time.

Hope was birthed in my childhood because I chose to see the blue sky, separate that I was different from the adults that had chosen destructive paths, and I chose to believe in a Higher Power. This hope grew into a tangible hope in foster care when my beloved foster mother cared for me, accepted and loved me, and took me to a summer camp for abused foster children called Royal Family Kids Camp (RFKC), where suddenly my entire life began to make sense as I became part of God's family, and with others that had survived abuse. A young lady named Jillian shared her testimony that she was abandoned and abused but found her home in God, the family of God. She shared that God was her *Abba* (the Aramaic word for Father, another name for God), and she began to cling to her Heavenly Father, who was always there for her. I witnessed this and was so moved. I did not grow up with a Father, but I saw this bond and connection as something inspiring. God *saw* me go through every unimaginable trauma as a young child. He believed me, saw value in me, and created me for something greater than trauma. He was *Abba* to me, and this was a new experience for me where I felt seen and valued for the first time. I had no idea this was possible.

Roughly thirteen years later, I became reconnected with the foster children's camp RKFC and came back as a camp counselor. At that time, I shared my story with the foster children and sang this impactful song called: *More Than Anything,* by *Point of Grace.*[6]

> God loves people more than anything.
> God loves people more than anything.
> More than anything He wants them to know

---

[6]   Point of Grace. "More Than Anything." Genius.com. June 1, 2023.

> He wants them to know
> He'd rather die than let them go
> 'Cause God loves people more than anything.
> God loves the weary
> When they're too weak to try
> He feels their pain, He knows their shame
> He cries with those who cry
> He won't give up or walk away
> When other people do
> 'Cause God loves people more than anything

As I shared my story, several foster boys came up to me and said, "I want to be just like you. Come back to RFKC and share my story!" My heart melted. This was the first time I had responded to God calling me to share my story with foster children and camp leaders, and I felt awestruck by their response. I was so nervous to speak in front of a couple hundred people, and I had no idea what to expect. I just knew these kids needed to hear that they were not alone. I had survived foster care and abuse, and they will too.

The truth became more apparent to me that God is *hope*. He can use our pain and our suffering to help others and provide encouragement and hope through becoming deeply connected to a loving, Heavenly Father. These foster children needed a tangible hope in God through my story (and by the way, I grew up with an intense fear of public speaking, and God still used my struggles!).

Isaiah 61:1 (NLT) says,

> The Spirit of the Sovereign Lord is upon me, for the Lord has anointed me to bring good news to the poor. He has sent me to comfort the brokenhearted and to proclaim that captives will be released and prisoners freed.[7]

---

[7]   Isaiah 61:1 (New Living Translation)

At another time, the Lord spoke compassion and purpose in me through speaking Joel 2:25,27 (NLT),

> The Lord says, "I will give you back what you lost to the swarming locusts, the hopping locusts, the stripping locusts, and the cutting locusts…Then you will know that I am among my people Israel, that I am the Lord your God, and there is no other. Never again will my people be disgraced."[8]

God's compassion is seen in Isaiah 30:18 (NIV),

> Yet the Lord longs to be gracious to you; therefore, He will rise up to show you compassion. For the Lord is a God of justice. Blessed are all who wait for Him![9]

Isaiah 54:10 (NIV),

> "Though the mountains be shaken and the hills be removed, yet my unfailing love for you will not be shaken nor my covenant of peace be removed," says the Lord who has compassion.[10]

God brings comfort through relationships. He shows compassion when we are hurt, and He wants to replace the hurt with healing and gladness. He longs to bring justice to the hurt we have encountered. God longs to show you where *seeds of hope, the birthplace of hope, have* sprung up in your life from the beginning to the present. He longs to reveal where He sprouted moments of *purpose and meaning* in the midst of loss and despair, where *peace and comfort*

---

[8] Joel 2: 25 & 27 (New Living Translation)
[9] Isaiah 30:18 (New International Version)
[10] Isaiah 54:10 (New International Version)

and the ability to keep going are semblances of His hand in your life as you bootstrapped your way through work every day, or cancer treatments, or going from foster home to foster home, wandering and feeling lost. He never lost sight of you. He is here right now.

It is easy to focus on all the bad. We are wired to easily see the things that are mismatched or incongruent, imperfect relationships, words misspoken, conversations when people missed you, or just when life seemed like it was not going right. It is easy to see the world through a "glass half empty" perspective. A *resilient and hope-filled posture* involves accepting the not-so-great on the one hand, but on the other hand accepting your strengths and who you are today, with all the progress you have made, and simultaneously moving forward. Does this feel hard to imagine?

Moment of reflection

Your story is still being written. The best part is you have the pen in your hand and the vision in your mind, and you were created for a purpose, so there are endless possibilities. Imagine holding a jar of memories in one hand that depicts your missteps and growth edges; imagine in the other hand holding a jar of memories that depict your progress, and your growth spurts. Now bring them together in your mind, and imagine accepting that you have both beautiful imperfections and progress with wonderful growth and resilience in you. One without the other would mean missing the learning and all you have overcome in order to be here today. Sometimes the scars can show the healing and the pain—but also the bravery to endure the hardship. Warriors are not made overnight.

So how do we rise up instead of giving up and embrace a hopeful future? It starts with being mindful in the moment of what is and accepting it presently in the state without judgment or expectation. This is mindfulness awareness. For instance, when I see a sunset, notice the wind, or I inhale and exhale out of my lungs, and I hear the purring sounds of a cat comfortably lying on my lap, this is being mindfully aware. Next is choosing gratitude. This is willfully looking at something with thankfulness and appreciation. For example, noticing that I am grateful I have working lungs and heart beating and that I woke up this morning. I am grateful I have the gift of life today. I have food to eat, clothing to wear, and a working vehicle (at the moment). Believing in the possibility and potential of yourself and a situation, even with the terrifying unknown. Believing that the answer will come and that I have the capacity to figure it out, and in God's timing, the door will open. I will not be left hanging. It is this cognitive process that is strength-filled and hope-based, speaking positively, courageously, moving forward, watching and experiencing the flow in life, or pausing in life. Believing I am a child of God and embracing that I am bringing my best self that I know forward, I will continue walking forward, reassuring myself that I will be okay. Recognizing that because I am alive and breathing at this moment, there is a possibility. Even while tied up in a trash bag inside the back of a car, I felt a sense of fear and the unknown, but I chose to focus on the fact that I could breathe and was still miraculously alive.

Rising up involves sacrificially giving oneself to others, even while going through one's own struggles and pain, and seeing the good potential in others, encouraging others, even while feeling discouraged. This involves countering the natural response, which is to see the negative and make excuses why not to get out of bed, but instead tap into the imagination and curiosity, listening, and rise up and get out of bed, even while struggling. Rising up entails being in the present moment instead of numbing out, remaining mindfully aware, and embracing what is in the current reality. For instance, this means acknowledging I feel sad, then sitting in it long enough to accept the sadness, and then telling myself, "It makes sense why I feel sad, because—" then saying, "—but it's normal to feel sad given that this happened. Others would feel sad too." Honoring how you feel dispels the stigma power emotions can have over you. For example, just by acknowledging the elephant in the room, you disempower any negative power or toxicity the emotions may have over you. This means that instead of ignoring the anxiety building up in my stomach, I acknowledge it is there, notice it, and release its power over me. This gives me the freedom to choose what to do with the anxiety in my stomach. These processes take time and require patient attention, shared experiences with others who have understanding, acceptance, and grace are tuned into, offer empathy and courage which comes from the heart. It is a process that unfolds, one tender moment at a time. Beauty springing forth from ashes requires such intention of the heart, soul, and mind, but then allows the painter to personalize the palette of colors, to rebirth and renew the beauty that was aching from the soul of the canvas to burst forth. This is a new beginning.

When I was seven, I made a conscious choice to understand the monsters in my life, to accept they chose to use their power for evil and harming others, and instead I chose to embrace, tremendous will, and faith I had survived. You do not have to have it all figured out at once, but remember, just enough faith can move mountains (Mark 11:23).[11] I had the curiosity and the core belief that *I must have survived for a purpose.* Two years later, God directly spoke to me that I was His child, and He removed me from the terror of living with my biological mother at seven and a half. God brought the police officers that arrested my biological mother as a direct intervention to scoop me up and out of the terror I was stuck in. I was then placed in foster care due to severe abuse and neglect, and she lost her parental rights. Since that terror, I can tell you that the birthplace of hope, when I was seven, looking out of the hotel room was just the beginning. Since then, I sought out opportunities and have witnessed God's golden threads of *Hope, Purpose, and Calling* woven into my life and identity at very integral times of my life. This solidified my identity in God as His daughter. If you are reading this now, whatever you have survived, no matter where you are in your life, God is here with you, and He desires to show you and have you experience His Hope from the Ashes. He wants you to know you are loved and valuable, no matter how you have been treated.

A researcher I admire, Dr. Brene Brown, states, "Wholehearted living is about engaging in our lives from a place of worthiness. I am enough. I am also brave and worthy of love and belonging. Love and belonging are irreducible needs of all men, women, and children. We're hardwired for connection. It's what gives purpose and meaning

---

[11] Mark 11:23 (New Living Translation).

to our lives. The absence of love, belonging, and connection always leads to suffering."[12] Our physiological brain is created for connection, and without it, we cannot thrive. Studies of babies in orphanages that are not experiencing positive stimulation, nurture, safety, being lovingly held, and having basic survival needs met, cannot survive. Through various people impacting my life, my brain became rewired such that I began seeing that I am worthy, I do belong, and I see and feel the connection through the love and gestures of others. My faith in God informed me that "…with God, all things are possible" (Matthew 19:26, NIV).[13] Through seasons of despair and loss, terror and triumph, I have believed that God is able, and so I leaned into Him and those He surrounded me with for support. Now I look back, and I believe that hope was born long before that moment when I was six years old and looking out the window, longing for something to rescue me. At that moment of Hope, I had experienced a God ordained moment where He captured my attention through the beauty of His creation and tugged on my heartstrings. He continues to weave His golden threads of Hope, healing, and redemption in my life, and I feel the goosebump moments of God working in my life. God will do any work to capture your attention. He shows up even in the little things if you look for Him and believe.

---

[12] Dr. Brene Brown, *Daring Greatly: How the Courage to Be Vulnerable Transforms the Way we Live, Love, Parent, and Lead* (England: Penguin Books, 2012), 10–11.

[13] Matt. 19:26 (New International Version).

CHAPTER 3

Bridging the Gaps

What you have experienced, no power on earth can take from you.
—Viktor E. Frankl, author of
Man's Search for Meaning[14]

Welcome back. This chapter will explore what may help provide a safety net and extension when what was needed was missing. As you dig into these chapters, remember to go at your own pace. Be kind to yourself and gentle to your soul. Perhaps you or others you know have endured hardships. Some of these stories may be difficult to read. Remember that the story of my life will not stay in pain but will show you how I passed through it. Hope is on the horizon.

Going from the heat of the fire into the sudden, harsh heat of the frying pan and back was incredibly difficult, and I longed for relief from the scorching heat. I was emotionally and psychologically tortured, physically ravaged, and utterly exhausted. Hanging by a mere thread, I kept wondering how in the world I would endure yet another round of abuse, the heartache that my flesh and blood mother would allow and initiate, and living in the bitter reality of constant trauma and loss of my childhood. My innocence was taken over and again, my integrity and value diminished, my imagination was hard pressed, and my heart felt crushed between the darkness.

---

[14] Viktor E. Frankl, *Man's Search for Meaning* (Boston: Beacon Press, 2006), 82.

My current reality was that the world had a gray, dull tint, and terror lurking at every corner. A dear professor of mine used to say that there existed two types of paranoia: one that was unfounded, not based on real threats but misperceptions, and the other was adaptive paranoia—one that became shaped due to *real* exposure to danger and threats. I had an adaptive paranoia that helped keep me alive, as I was acutely perceptive of the dangers around me in constantly fighting double and triple binds to survive.

Apparently, my hypervigilance for the surrounding danger was adaptive so that I could use it as an asset to remain safer, knowing what would please my perpetrators. I grew accustomed to flying under the radar, noting what was happening and by whom, and anticipating what would happen next. I saw that if someone was non-compliant, they would be forced to endure inhumane, degrading torture—that is the ugly, stark reality of the human trafficking culture. You do *anything* to survive, and your senses are constantly heightened, or else, you are at risk of suffering greatly. Thus, I lived in a state of intensified anxiety and hypervigilance. I was not acquainted with peace. I lived on the edge for much of my earlier life and even as I grew up because it became so hardwired. This is similar to how Veterans returning from war try to adapt to civilian life after exposure to war-torn areas where they were fighting for their life and the lives of others. Trauma reshapes the brain's wiring system and is adaptive to circumstances and situations for survival. As a result, the brain can learn to be on overdrive, triggered easily (like feeling startled or reliving trauma when fireworks are displayed). Then the brain becomes accustomed to not knowing how to turn the heightened survival switch off when no longer in severe danger. How was I to move on and feel safe or even feel normal with such exposures? It is not like I could start over or pretend that nothing had happened to me. I was living in a nightmare and could not escape, though I tried twice.

Often, people would ask what it was like for me growing up, and most of the time, I would remain silent, listening to their stories (while trying so hard to imagine what it would look like to live a life of adventure and joy without being terrorized or trafficked), and redirect them by asking them questions about their life, and altogether avoiding my own life story. I did not want to overwhelm anyone and did not want to be judged, criticized, or misunderstood, so I remained silent. Meanwhile, I felt so alone. Other times, I was an open book about some details and either received blank stares or quick hugs with, "I'm sure you'll be fine. You're strong." These dismissive statements reinforced that I was *different* from others and alone. For a long time, I resorted to remaining silent. My shoulders drooped lower. *Sigh.* "But it's not that simple!" I would say in my head. "No one understands me. How can I trust anyone?" How could I know the threats my mom spoke the last time she saw me at Orangewood Children's Home at age seven were not possible—that she may not be able to find me and try to kill me, as she said she would if I told anyone what had happened to me. I was left alone in utter sadness, trying to figure out the reality of life and who I was. My soul was crushed. I felt invisible and like I did not matter.

The greatest "gap" I experienced was the lack of a protector in my life. I desperately wanted someone to swoop in and carry me out of the danger. I longed to be saved and told that it would all be okay. Like Maid Marian in *Robin Hood, Prince of Thieves*, I wanted a rescuer.[15] And not just any rescuer, a dramatic rescuer—one that would bring justice to all the injustice I had experienced as a little girl. I wanted to be seen, held, and nurtured. Sadly, I often felt stuck and wondered if it would ever end. It is true that I am an expert at life's tidal waves, as I endured several in my life. As a former surfer, competitive swimmer, and lifeguard, I was well-acquainted with the dangers and juxtaposing thrill of the ocean. I watched the conditions and kept track of the people—over-anticipating challenges. I could handle the predictable challenges, but when it came to less predictable tsunamis or incessant tidal waves, I would freeze and feel immediately overwhelmed, and then the "*s*" word would surface—I was *stuck* like I was in a cage. I could relate to *Jane Eyre* as she felt

---

[15] *Robinhood Prince of Thieves*, directed by Kevin Reynolds (Morgan Creek Productions, Warner Bros, 1991), 2:23.

like a bird in a cage trying to be freed.[16] I longed to be set free, once and for all.

It is possible to overuse your adrenaline, and it takes years to restore. The amygdala in my brain has a "stuck gas pedal," overfiring due to the tremendous life-threatening stress I had to endure on a daily basis. I lived in complex trauma for such a long period. I could not find a way to calm my brain down. All I knew was feeling anxious and being in survival mode. Have you ever experienced the over-revving of a vehicle and come to find out the gas tank is empty and the vehicle is out of fuel? That is the image of our adrenaline—used in small doses, mini-crises, and selective challenges. It is manageable, serves its purpose, and can reboot. However, in large doses, it puts the body in overdrive and depletes our resources. I needed a lifeline to protect my peace and calm my mind, body, and emotions, and I needed it fast. My adrenaline was shot, and I was depleted.

My lifelines have changed throughout my life. But the steadfast ones during tough seasons were people I could safely confide in, friendships, family, faith, therapists, eating healthy, exercise, chocolate, and sometimes Netflix. One area I struggled with was relaxing. I never learned how to fully enter a relaxation state, and with my history, getting massages was not my first choice. After I had done more therapy work and trauma processing, I learned how much trauma was stored in my body, that I needed to do bodywork to reconnect with myself; trust that my body is my ally in healing, and practice deep breathing, progressive relaxation, Pilates, massages, physical therapy, dance, running, and other ways to ground myself and reconnect with my body.

Moment of reflection

What have you used as your lifeline to help you bridge the gaps? I imagine work, beer, or wine at Happy Hour to blow off steam, food or sweets, sex, money, power, anything that distracts, or what about support from family or friends, faith, exercise, etc. What are areas you can

------

[16] Charlotte Bronte, *Jane Eyre* (England: Wordsworth, 1996).

grow in to reconnect with yourself in healthy ways and reconnect with truth? Take a moment to pause and think about how your current or past lifelines were serving you. Were they adding to your life and being beneficial? If so, take a moment to celebrate that. If not, take a moment to revise your lifelines and write out what you could do instead to add to your life. Remember, you are worth it and deserve a wholesome life that nurtures your mind, body, and soul.

How can bridging the gap occur? What does that mean? First, it involves faith and trust in the possibility that something can help, benefit, and cover a series of needs that could not otherwise be met without intervention. For example, I needed to have faith that there could be an alternative person who could step in and peacefully support me without critical remarks. Second, it involves surrender. Counter-intuitive, right? Surrender involves holding enough faith and trust to let go of what is unhelpful and a belief that better can come by releasing than holding tighter. This took a while for me to understand because I lived in chaos and always felt zero sense of control, along with experiencing a great deal of loss. Surrender became an essential part of my healing process and, over time, became easier (with reminders!). Third, bridging the gap involves being honest with yourself about what is missing and what your limitations are and that these limitations are not necessarily a bad thing. I needed to recognize the innocence, bravery, and strength that was preserved from my childhood were *positive protective mechanisms* and simultaneously that I also had blind spots since I was not mirrored by my biological mother. There were some things I needed to accept were missing. Accepting these imperfections and embracing my limitations made room for me to grow and feel less stuck. Fourth, while I was growing, I needed an essential ingredient to bridge the gap for what was missing: *grace.*

For instance, when I would misstep, instead of believing the voice of shame, I would offer myself grace, forgiveness instead of feeling stuck in guilt, and self-compassion rather than being self-critical. This took me a great deal of time, even into my doctoral program in my mid to late thirties, as I did not know there was a different way of being. I often felt that exceedingly high expectations were put on me, and I frequently felt stressed or overburdened with trying to figure it out by myself. This would lead to burnout and feeling "less than." Part of this came from being a parentified child, meaning as a young child, there was a role reversal where I cared for my biological mom with a mental illness rather than her take care of me. I knew nothing more than taking care of others, but I felt rewarded by doing something good. Was this a flaw? Or was this how my environment shaped me despite my emotional, physical, and developmental needs not being met? Every so often, I have a moment where I can sense I am not getting something, and I feel uneasy. Fifth, I have learned to trust my intuition, gather information, ask questions, and make my best conclusions. After all, that is all we can do—to try our best. Remember these steps in bridging the gap for what you have endured. These are essential if you want to attain more freedom, healing, and peace from what you have survived. I found resources and experts to help me with these steps. It is possible to walk through and find healing and growth. I have.

Growth comes in micro-movements, inches, steps, or even spurts. I often would have microgrowth experiences where I could not "see myself" and how I was growing until I hit a growth spurt. For instance, when I was eleven years old, I grew three shoe sizes in one summer! Then, I stopped growing. Boy, did my feet hurt! Emotionally, psychological, and spiritually, I grew the same way in microsteps or spurts. As I reflect, I wish it had been modeled for me that it is okay to grow this way; it is neither good nor bad; it is how I am. Acceptance, self-compassion, love, and grace are the ideal formula for engaging with bridging the gaps in your life. Remember, those gaps are often there not because of you but because someone else did not do their own work of healing in their life and negatively impacted you. *Maybe you have felt shame or discouragement that you disappointed someone, or could not measure up, or felt enough—that is the absence of love and nurturing, not the lacking in you.* Being able to authentically define yourself, see yourself as you really are, and separate yourself from other's messages spoken into your life, will enable you to make more space in your life for bridging the gaps.

Powerful encounters with people or God have miraculously shaped who I am, and they helped fill the gaps or bridge them. A theme I have noticed in my life is that different individuals have shown up at every season of my life in an impactful way. These are goose bump moments that bring me such joy and confirmation that I really do matter. To this day, this still astounds me! In particular, my foster mom came in and out of my life at two different times over the course of a year and a half. I can look back and see big parts of that experience have contributed to who I am today…determined and steadfast. She would sit with me while I struggled in school trying to learn how to read, write, do math, and make friends. She would believe in me and say, "You can do this! Keep working hard, and you can do it!" By fourth grade, while working with my foster mom, I had finally earned my first A. I look back and see how God had brought other mentors and angels into my life, from church pastors and wives, chaperones, friends, or random people I met wherever I was; these people rose up to strengthen and encourage me, for which I am deeply grateful. In other instances, such as at Royal Family Kids Camp (RFKC), there was a camp photographer who was always there uplifting the kids, and he put together our camp photo books. It was and is my first memory book, my "baby album."

This incredible act of service impacted me greatly. I later reconnected and thanked him for what he did. This photo book defined an important part of my identity and was positive! Little did I know, seeing him and telling him how the photo book shaped my life also impacted his life! He had told me that he was going through a hard time when he volunteered at the camps as a photographer, and he did not know if he was making a difference. I told him that I still have my memory book and how much it meant to me to have pictures from my earlier childhood. I pulled it out of my purse at that moment and showed it to him—He had tears in his eyes. As it turned out, God used him to bring joy into my life as a foster child and in many hundreds of other kids' lives. But it did not stop there—God used me in his life too! This impactful experience came full circle. We often do not get to see the imprints we make on others' lives and how their lives turn out; that day was different. RFKC was ahead of its time in how it instilled hope and resilience in young foster youth. Today, in light of current research, I can trace back what the camp developers envisioned and produced and see how much they really understood the needs of foster youth and how it shaped me and impacted my resilience. I have, in turn, used those experiences and knowledge to help others, bringing it full circle. You can do this too! Dear friends and family, through the years, have made imprints too. The main influence, however, was God. Every moment I felt stuck, alone, or purposeless, God showed up, provided truth, reflected my identity, and reminded me I am part of His family, I am valuable and loved, and I have a purpose. Seeds of hope began to sprout throughout my life.

Moment of reflection

God uses anyone willing to bridge the gap for the needs of love, acceptance, belonging, redemption, peace, growth, and resilience. It can happen through a composed song, a word of encouragement, a smile, a commitment to the greater good of society, and patience to sit with the outcasts of society and show love through giving of yourself. What could you do for someone else that may positively impact their life? How can you step out of your "comfort zone" to show love and bring support to those in need? Even if you have not started or finished your healing work, God can still use you right where you are.

The funny thing about *Bridging the Gaps* is it does not become evident until you are able to see the forest through the trees. Believing in *possibility* was the tallest task and required the greatest perseverance and strength. It is easy to give up when circumstances are turning downward. Sometimes moments of grace and truth sprout up, providing a breath of fresh air, new perspective, meaning in the moment, and the will to keep on going. My life has revealed a series of bridges between hardships, losses, and trauma, and without these bridges, I do not know where I would be. I am grateful for all the bridges because they have kept the spark of hope alive for me throughout my entire life and fueled me to press on and be a bridge for others.

There's a famous poem written by Robert Frost from 1916 that captures the essence of embracing the bridges we cross amid suffering, entitled *The Road Not Taken*:[17]

> Two roads diverged in a yellow wood,
> And sorry I could not travel both
> And be one traveler, long I stood
> And looked down one as far as I could
> To Where it bent in the undergrowth;
> Then took the other, as just as fair,
> And having perhaps the better claim,
> Because it was grassy and wanted wear;
> Though as for that the passing there
> Had worn them really about the same,
> And both that morning equally lay
> In leaves no step had trodden black.
> Oh, I kept the first for another day!
> Yet knowing how way leads on to way,
> I doubted if I should ever come back.
> I shall be telling this with a sigh
> Somewhere ages and ages hence;
> Two roads diverged in a wood, and I—
> I took the one less traveled by,
> And that has made all the difference.

Each of us comes to a fork in the road at one point in our life. We wish we could, in fact, travel both roads and discover which is the best path to take, but we are not given that option. We often struggle with doubt and anguish in not knowing which is the right way to go in life. In the end, the road less traveled was what illuminated my path and paved the path I was supposed to go. I had to continue journeying in faith, belief, and trust that good was coming.

---

[17] Robert Frost, *The Road Not Taken: A Selection of Robert Frost's Poems* (New York: H. Holt and Co, 1991).

Moment of reflection

Have you experienced life seemingly taking you on one path, and you find yourself utterly confused, shocked, or in despair? Or you find two paths, both seem equally wonderful, and you step on one path and discover it is not what you expected? Or rather, you took a leap of faith and discovered an amazing path! There is risk in walking by faith. We try to convince ourselves that we really know the right path to take when, in fact, we want a path that is free from pain, chaos, stress, or loss. I have been down a similar path where I felt so frozen in time and just wanted to know what was the right path. I did not want to make a mistake or repeat the past. What job should I take? What school is good for kids? What doctor do I see? Where do I live? Whom should I marry? What's my next step in treating my health? Faith and trusting your intuition, guidance from others, and stepping forward are what needs to happen to witness how it may unfold. It is risky and vulnerable but necessary. I invite you to journal or write down thoughts about the paths you have taken, what it was like, and how you felt. Then take a bird's-eye view and see where it brought you to later. What did you gain? What did you lose? What would you do differently? Or what would you celebrate in what you tried to do (practice grace and self-compassion)? What about the journey and the path(s) made a difference for you?

Growing up making several adultlike decisions at a very tender age, I became accustomed to the art of decision-making, but the stress never lessened. I grew up with an intensity and heaviness that I always had to know what to do or if something was wrong with me. I had gaps in having models for what my role should be and how to do certain things. As a child, after all, the decisions I was faced with were overwhelming and filled with confusion, such as picking between double binds of safety and picking the answer to challenges such as why did my mother abuse me and leave me? Why was I not sought after when I was missing for five and a half years or protected from the perpetrators? Why was I taken away from my foster mother, who was going to adopt me? Why was I without a family until I was adopted at twelve? Why did previous relationships end with feeling unloved and alone?

Why did I receive a severe diagnosis of stenosis and scoliosis, leaving me to deal with severe nerve pain and no cure? Why did I have another near-death experience with emergency surgery for my appendix? This all added more layers of traumatic stress in my adult years, while at the same time, my problem-solving strategies ran dry. I had an empty well. The truth was, I bore the responsibility for other people's decisions in my life that were not mine and even the "why" in things that happened. I had convinced myself since I was eventually moved off the streets and put in foster care, that if I was "good enough" and did the "right thing," nothing else bad would happen. Then I would be loved and cared for, and the bad men and the terrorizing situations from my early childhood would never happen again. I figured if I took the blame, it would some-how be "fixed." But as I grew up, complex situations became more complex. Where were the bridges? Where were the caring people, opportunities, angels, and mentors that showed up before? We shall explore this further. Sometimes in the midst of unresolved situations and people, I learned the best thing is accepting the other party had their own brokenness and wounds, and that I would need to grieve the loss and pain I had experienced, and maybe answers as to "why" would come later but only God knows.

A favorite high school novel I read was *Jane Eyre*, which depicted a young orphan girl who grew up feeling like a bird in a cage.[18] I could relate to her immediately as a foster child and feeling stuck in a cage, with my wings clipped back and no idea about what freedom was. A quote of Jane's was, *"I remember that the real world was wide and that a varied field of hopes and fears, of sensations, and excitements, awaited those who had the courage to go forth into its expanse, to seek real knowl-edge of life amidst its perils."*[19] The key was *courage*. The willingness to taste and see, explore and discover, laugh and cry, was the bridge. Dr.

---

[18] Charlotte Bronte, *Jane Eyre* (England: Wordsworth, 1996).
[19] Charlotte Bronte, *Jane Eyre* (England: Wordsworth, 1996), 2.

Brene Brown, who studied shame resilience in women and wrote *The Gifts of Imperfection*, speaks of courage in this way:[20]

> Courage is a heart word. The root of the word Courage is *Cor*—the Latin word for *Heart*. In one of its earliest forms, the word *courage* had a very different definition than it does today. Courage originally meant "to speak one's mind by telling all one's heart." Over time, this definition has changed, and today, courage is more synonymous with being *heroic*. Heroics is important and we certainly need heroes, but I think we've lost touch with the idea that speaking honestly and openly about who we are, about what we're feeling, and about our experiences (good and bad) is the definition of *courage*. Heroics is often about putting our life on the line. Ordinary courage is about putting our vulnerability on the line. In today's world, that's pretty extraordinary.

Having a compass to guide and bring truth in the midst of life's challenges can be a breath of fresh air and sometimes a lifeline. *Courage*, indeed, is a compass. Without courage, random acts of kindness would not occur. Without courage, our military would not fight for good. Without courage, we would not be here today—you would not be here reading this book. You are a fighter and have weathered many storms. Courage is a tool that has helped you come far.

Moment of reflection

Can you think back to when you first discovered courage and gave it a try? When was the next time you were courageous? How did it feel

---

[20] Brene Brown, *I Thought It Was Just Me (But It Isn't): Making the Journey From "What Will People Think?" to "I Am"* (New York: Penguin Publishing Group, 2007), 266–267.

when you were courageous? Scary or empowering? Noting these moments throughout your life is key in linking the pieces of your story, including the bridges that have assisted you this far and the next chapter of your journey.

Against all odds, courageous people find hope, meaning, and purpose in the midst of dire circumstances. Courage is tied to resilience. We will venture down this road shortly. But before we do, let's tie this together. In this chapter, I have shared integral pieces of my story. I have been brave in being transparent with you in hopes that you can know you are not alone, and it takes courage to grow in your life and make a difference in others' lives. Others have gone through tough times and are still breathing. We discussed discovering seeds of hope in the midst of life's tragedies and seeing them sprout and create links of illuminating hope to keep going in your life. We explored steps of bridging the gap, which include clinging to faith and trust in possibility, surrender, being honest with what may be missing in your life and limitations, accepting your imperfections, embracing your limitations, offering yourself grace, forgiveness, and self-compassion instead of the negative messages, and trusting your intuition as you venture down the road less traveled. These gaps may take on different forms. They can be growing up with an absent parent, one who is abusive or an alcoholic, a severe mental illness, drug addiction, foster care, job loss, marital stress, financial stress, natural disasters, medical challenges like cancer or a heart attack, car accidents, the loss of a baby, and the list goes one. Bridging the gap involves taking a reflective look at what you can do when your needs are just as real as the pain you have endured. Also, remember to celebrate micro-to-massive growth as it becomes evident in your life. Hope springs forth with these bridges and your growth.

My greatest bridge has been leaning into God and letting Him hold me. Without God in my life, I would not be standing on two feet and writing this story to you. I owe the very breath in my lungs, every heartbeat, to Him. It had taken every ounce of energy to keep moving forward when I felt like all was lost when my life was threatened several times as a young child, and I felt stuck with no hope.

It has taken tremendous grit, strength, and resilience to trust that because God allowed me to survive near starvation, severe abuse, and complex trauma, I was created for a purpose, and He was going to get me through this, no matter what! I could hardly fathom how deep, wide, and grand God's love is for me. I had to practice receiving it and holding onto it. This was a new experience for me. Every day I thank Him and am humbled. Resilience is the ability to bounce back after challenges and extreme trauma and difficulties. It is the part of you that says, "No! I'm not giving up! There has to be a way!" With God, *all* things are possible.

CHAPTER 4

The Warrior Is a Child

You may not control all the events that happened to
you, but you can decide not to be reduced by them.
Try to be a rainbow in someone's cloud.

—Mary Angelou, author of
Letter to My Daughter[21]

Maya Angelou was a warrior and a resilient survivor. She endured horrid sexual abuse at the young age of seven, and when a family member took the perpetrator's life, she became mute for years. A lover of books and creative works, she began speaking again at age twelve and then took off with writing poetry, singing, dancing, acting, and much more.[22] At her heart, Maya Angelou was a warrior.

For those of us that have endured great trials in our lives, perseverance is key to pulling through. However, there may be setbacks along the way when life becomes overwhelming. These setbacks can become comebacks if you keep a healthy perspective or remember to jump back on the train of life if you fall off. To become a warrior, you are likely unaware of how much you fought to survive and are just grateful to have breath in your lungs. Humility is often a trait

---

[21] Maya Angelou, *Letter to my Daughter* (New York: Random House Publishing, 2009), xii.

[22] Maya Angelou, *"Maya Angelou"* (Poetry Foundation, June 1, 2023), https:// www.poetryfoundation.org/poets/maya-angelou.

of a warrior. They have shed blood, sweat, and tears; have physical and emotional scars, aches, and pains; but they get back up. The key to resilience is having great courage and undaunting willingness, as Viktor Frankl did, to look past the darkness and see a vision of hope, gratitude, and purpose in pain, even when he encountered the greatest human suffering while spending three years in Nazi concentration camps.[23]

Do you ever find yourself admiring the soldiers that are deployed out to combat in their military garb? Or characters in movies that are dressed for battle on their noble steeds, with shields polished and swords reflective like mirrors? These warriors risk their life for others and march or run into battle, knowing full well the dangers ahead, but with the knowledge and skills they have readily prepared themselves with. So what happens when life becomes a battleground? How do we manage to march into it with the same confidence? Or do you run away? Mock the danger? Or blame yourself for the problem at hand? This chapter will dive into one of the hardest realizations of human nature—we are wired for struggle, we are created to deal with difficulties, but sometimes they are so great, so unexpected, they knock us down. Then, what do we do?

Twila Paris wrote a song entitled "The Warrior Is a Child."[24] In it, she depicts a wounded girl hit left and right with difficulties. Though strong and amazing, she hides her tears. Eventually, she goes home and is picked up by her Heavenly Father as she weeps before God. Inside each of us is a warrior, fit for battle, hidden behind armor. It could be an armor of protection, of success, a mask of comedy, or drunken sadness. As a child and through my adult years, I tried to be real, but only as far as I felt I could, then I would wear the armor of being invisible. This was familiar. I grew up around psychopaths and sociopaths who used intimidation and fear to control and berate those around them. I learned quickly that I had to be thinking ten steps ahead of them before every move I made. I was a chameleon by nature, blending into any and every situation so as not to stand

---

[23] Viktor E. Frankl, *"Man's Search for Meaning"* (Boston: Beacon Press, 2006).
[24] Twila Paris, "The Warrior Is a Child," Genius.com, June 1, 2023.

out. Stay small, quiet, calm, and hide. When faced with life or death, or even chaos, street smarts were the only tool I had to live. Hiding in spaces no one would fit, in corners, crouched low, under the bed, behind pillows, in cupboards. I knew to "play dumb" and pretend to know nothing—then no one felt challenged or intimidated. I listened acutely to every sound, breath, tone, wind, car, and movement. I imagined where things were strategically placed in a room and pictured it over and over in my head with my eyes closed. I would map out escape routes if I ever got free. I was trapped in the hands of a sociopath, my biological mother, and evil men. If I ever broke free, the plan would have to be fool proof. I would have to be quick and swiftly silent. Virtually undetectable. Awake at night, silent by day. However, if I failed, it could mean ending my life. I was in a serious fight for my life.

One night, when I was two years old, my biological mother was in one of her erratic rages, talking to herself. She threw me into a closet under the stairs in the dark. I sat there for a day. Oddly enough, I felt peace under those stairs—I was far away from her. One night, I felt lonely and quietly nudged the door open, sliding the chair that was blocking it away, and tiptoed to my room. I grabbed my small, soft teddy bear. I quickly slid the chair and closed the door. I held onto my comforting teddy bear with all my strength. I told him that it would be okay and I would take care of him. Then my moment of peace passed, and she barged into the room, yanking my arm. I had my bear in the grasp of my other arm. She tried to pull him away. I held tighter. I wish I hadn't—his arm tore off. She threw him in a black trash bag with all my other things. I lay still on the bed thinking—at least he is in the bag. She can't hurt him. I became invisible to the abuser. Yet the emotional and psychological wounds were evident and came back in flashes of memories or in similar situations that reminded me of those incorrigible moments of rage, abuse, or neglect I experienced. I was told I was a wise, old soul, even as a little girl, strong and knowledgeable beyond my years. The truth is, I had to be to survive. I often cried myself to sleep—no home, no one to run to, no one to hold me. I lived in utter terror by day and by night. I was a warrior child survivor. I never had a quiet, safe place to rest. I was always vigilant of enemies, evil, or anything unsafe, lurking around the next stop or the next man that walked into our motel room; there was nowhere safe to turn. I wore invisible armor so that no one would hurt me like these monsters did. It took me a long time to trust and to learn that I do not have to trust right away—that trust is earned. It took a long time to learn that I had healthy, normal, adaptive paranoia because *real* danger and abuse had occurred.

It took me a long time to learn that nothing was *wrong* with me—it was the perpetrators that were sadistic, narcissistic, and toxic. It took a long time to learn that *I am lovable. I deserve to be cherished and loved and treated with value*, and what happened to me did not change the value that God created me with! Even after a deep loss, pain, and rejection from previous relationships, I had to relearn that I am lovable, deserving to be honored, cherished, valued, and protected. I had to learn that I do not attract unhealthy people; unhealthy individuals seek after those that are vulnerable, kind, caring, empathic, and sacrificial because they have their own insecurities that they put on others. They choose to use others to fill those insecurities. I had to learn how to set boundaries with those that were kind but manipulative or had subtleties that blurred the lines of what is healthy in relationships. I had to learn to be okay with being a female and put down the sword of self-protection with those that are safe, loving, and within the inner circle that I choose. All this took time because, deep down, the warrior is a child, and she wore armor to survive the most horrific experiences of poverty, starvation, violence, physical and sexual trauma, and loss of freedom. She was human trafficked and used as bait to lure other men. She became use to being used, and she was unaware of the impact of being used— that is, became her blind spot. She was alone and fearful, wondering if she would survive.

The warrior is a child—she became self-aware, detecting danger immediately, reading people, and learning how to combat the double binds of survival between near-death experiences and severe abuse. She was learning lessons she was too young to learn. It was at that time the birth of a caregiver came out in me. Under those solemn stairs, locked away from her mother, the monster, the little warrior in me, cared for that teddy bear like she wanted to be cared for and protected. That was the last time I saw a toy until foster care at seven and a half or eight years of age. Another feature birthed—the fighter in me. I wanted to protect my bear and wanted to free her. I would sneak out and go to the pool, as mentioned previously, and I found solace in the water and in the strength I was building. At the same time, the child in me so earnestly wanted to be loved and held. My biological mother never held or loved me. In fact, when she found out she was pregnant with me, she pretended that she was not and refused to eat well or take care of herself. I became accustomed to not being valued.

When I was six or seven years old, my mother became pregnant by a terrible man who raped her. She began to grow a belly as the baby grew, and when she could not do her job as a prostitute, I was used instead by men. When she became about six months pregnant, she then tragically bled a lot, miscarrying the baby and throwing it into a trash can in the hotel in her mental illness state. I was in shock. At first, I thought she had killed the baby! Then with tears in my eyes and sadness in my heart, I realized this baby girl was my sister, and she would have never survived. Why am I here? There must be a purpose. How did I make it so far and I am still alive? I was born C-section—six weeks early. The umbilical cord was wrapped around my neck, and I almost died, but I had survived. I learned later that I had survived other near-death experiences. Another time I was drugged by the head human trafficker, and I was paralyzed. I felt so sick and scared. I was raped and assaulted and could not move, but I saw it all happen before my eyes. This occurred more than once. I learned later that if he had used a higher dose of date-rape-drug, I could have died—I was only a tiny child. When I witnessed my bio-logical mom miscarry, I was blamed for the baby's death and beaten as a result. If I had outlived my sibling and continued to survive this far, then I must be here for a purpose. There must be something greater—I thought at seven, staring out of the hotel window into the sunshine. I began to fight for my very existence, telling myself that this palpable pain and hardship, abuse and loss, had to occur for a

Higher meaning and purpose, or else, all I was left with was survivor's guilt, and it would all be meaningless.

The warrior in me also arose when I was seven years old while being trafficked. My mother was being drugged and beaten by this evil man while we were in Arizona, as he was ripping off her clothes. I was standing at the door. Something rose up inside me—I knew that my mom could not take care of herself or me. She was seeing things and hearing things and was ill with a psychotic disorder amid other psychological issues. So in my mind, as a little girl, it was *my* job to protect her and take care of her. I was her caregiver. She and I were completely homeless, and she had no job. Therefore, I felt the need to protect her from being treated so wrongly.

I confidently said to the evil man, "Leave her alone! Don't hurt her!"

He came up to me and threatened me with his gruff tone.

He said, "What did you say?"

I stared him in the eyes. "Leave her alone," I said sternly.

He grabbed me by the neck of my clothing and held me up high, dropped me down, and tore my clothes. Then the unthinkable happened. He chased me, like a game, around his apartment and began hitting me with beer bottles, making me call him "daddy," and physically assaulting me. By the end, he drugged me with a needle, and raped me, then stuffed me in a black trash bag. He punished me for not complying. This was the darkest of my memories and a night I've never forgotten. The next day, I remembered words that came out of my biological mother's mouth: "You're a slut." The next thing I knew, the man threw me into the back of his truck while I was still in the trash bag—such a symbol of how I felt, thrown out like trash. I did not matter to anyone. No one stopped him. I was worthless and unlovable. These beliefs tormented me for years but especially when I had not been adopted for years and had experienced a failed adoption. Where was I to go? Who would love me? Where do I belong? Somehow, the warrior inside me refused to give up. I was determined to keep going. There had to be a reason why I survived yet another tormenting and frightening event.

As I look back, I realize that I had survived the ultimate nightmare. I had thought out multiple escape plans, but my adrenaline ran so high that my heart and my voice spoke before my logic chimed in. I would have regretted not standing up for her, but I was still aware that this monster could have killed her and me. I chose to fight. I have been a warrior from the time I was born until the present. I still get stirred up when others are treated unjustly: babies, children, homeless, widows/widowers, single parents, divorced parents or children of divorced families, transgender, LGBTQ, racism, sexism, foster youth, or anyone mistreated. The fire for justice grew stronger.

The Bible talks about how God possesses righteous anger toward injustice and leaves no stone unturned for His children if any wrong is done to them. I hold to this truth at my core that one day, God will bring justice for all the wrongdoing in my life and in others. As a child, I grew into a warrior to survive and bring hope to others. This is what Jesus models for us—that He is a warrior fighting on our behalf.

I wrote this poem, depicting the battle within as I was dealing with the battle surrounding me growing up and throughout my life.

I am a warrior. I fight inside for what's right.

I am a warrior. I don't give in to what's not right.

I am a warrior. My heart bleeds for innocence torn.

I am a warrior. There's so much harm I mourn.

I am a warrior. I give, give, give and expect nothing

I am a warrior. I put others first, even with my heart aching.

I am a warrior. I've battled like a first responder.

I am a warrior. I lean on God, my Heavenly Father.

I am a warrior. I forget to rest; I want to be held and secure.

I am a warrior. I often feel alone in the test, but remember there's a door.

I am a warrior. I belong to God, my Abba.

I am a warrior. He keeps me strong while I sob and cry out, "Ah!"

I am a warrior. God is my teacher and miracle worker.

I am a warrior. I'm a survivor 'cause He's my sustainer.

Moment of reflection

You see, a big part of your story is in recognizing where it was the hardest, and then reaching out for help and tapping into healthy resources, and acknowledging that you, too, are a warrior. If you were not, you would not be here today, reading this with me, sharing my story, and realizing the significance of yours. What are encouraging, strong words you can say to yourself—with your losses, hardships, and pain—that can acknowledge you too are a warrior? Take a moment to pause now. This is an important piece in your healing, to admire the warrior inside you.

I have often wished on numerous occasions that I never had to endure the extreme hardship I experienced in my life. It was excruciating. But I tell you this, without a shadow of a doubt, I would not be a strong woman with grit, resilience, and be the fighter that I am today without the will to survive. My children have the opportunity to experience these qualities from me, and I can see them in my children. Now you may be thinking, "But I never had anyone show me or help me through my situation." I get that. It wasn't until my later years that I began seeing the connections and making sense of the messiness. Today, I can honestly say that I appreciate who I am, the growth I have made, and the realizations of truth I have come to as a result of creating meaning from difficulties. Remember that the past can inform the future for the rest of your life. Those are gems of truth, especially as you formulate meaning and purpose out of the pain of your past—that, my friends, is why we survive! This is not the end of your story! Thank goodness!

In my experience and my years of studies, I have come to realize that *God wants to redeem every piece that was broken, every earth-shattering stained-glass window, and transform it into a masterpiece.* Isaiah 43:1 and 4 says, "Do not fear, for I have redeemed you; I have called you by name; you are Mine... You are precious, and honored in My sight and I love you..."[25] What a beautiful promise! I consciously

---

[25] Isaiah 43:1 and 4 (Amplified).

chose to etch this truth into my heart. I bought an art piece depicting this beautiful reminder hanging on my wall right now. The warrior is the child within all of us. We just need to give him or her a voice, with extra comfort, and keep speaking the truth. You and your story matter. Second Chronicles 20:15 says, "Thus says the Lord to you: 'Do not be afraid nor dismayed because of this great multitude, for the battle is not yours, but God's.'"[26] Another great growth step of the warrior is to discern when they are to go to battle and when they need to rest and surrender. Picking our battles comes from utilizing wisdom and discernment. This takes practice recognizing that God is battling injustice on our behalf. He wants us to let Him do that because He cares for us. Exodus 14:14, "The Lord will fight for you while you [only need to] keep silent and remain calm."[27] In those moments when it is tempting to fret and worry about things, fear creeps in; trusting in God that He has you and staying calm in mind and heart is the safest thing. Embracing this verse can help. Trust me when I say this, the things I have learned, have been gleaned over time, with support, therapy, and reminders like these verses that God sees everything, and He is the ultimate warrior for us. Growth and progress take time. Be patient.

---

[26] Second Chronicles 20:15 (New King James Version).
[27] Exodus 14:14 (Amplified).

CHAPTER 5

Illumination
Light Shines Bright Even in the Darkness

Only when we know our own darkness well can we be
present with the darkness of others. Compassion becomes
real when we recognize our shared humanity.[28]

—Dr. Brene Brown

Welcome back, readers. If you have made it this far, you are halfway through this piece. I can imagine some of you are thinking—phew! Thank goodness! I'm not so sure how much more I can handle! Remember, you're a warrior. You've got this, and I'm right here beside you. I have lived it and have come out on the other side. Others might be thinking, wow, I am on the edge of my seat! But can I really grow into what I am reading and what I want to be? Absolutely! Keep persevering. Remember, we often journey through a season of awareness, imagination, and polishing before we can see the true beauty and luster of the stone or glass we're shaping and eventually viewing. Even with broken glass, light shines through it. Have you ever looked through a kaleidoscope? There are reflecting surfaces inside; when held up to the light, you see the most mesmerizing designs. This only happens through repeated reflection. Our lives are like kaleido-

---

28 Dr. Brene Brown, *Daring Greatly: How the Courage to Be Vulnerable Transforms the Way we Live, Love, Parent, and Lead* (England: Penguin Books, 2012), 234.

scopes. When light shines on them, and we reflect deeper and take time to appreciate beauty, triumph, tragedy, and tears, we can really be seen. Isn't that what we all desire? To be seen? Appreciated? Loved? Accepted? Known? I share with you these deep, heart needs. We all need to be held and told, "It will be okay. You will get through this, and I am here for you." But we live in a culture where there is often an absence of individuals that have enough emotional intelligence, time, or empathy to sit with us, truly understand us, and believe in us.

Moment of reflection

Even in your darkest hour, one sliver of light, like when the sun is setting below the ocean, is enough to illuminate everything in its path. Light shines bright even in darkness. Though we cannot see the wind, we can feel the effects of it if we really pay attention. We need these glimmers of hope, as God weaves His golden threads of truth throughout our life to illuminate our lives and bring us purpose and meaning. What can you honestly say is a glimmer of hope or spark of light that brought truth to a situation in your life? What would it look like to tap into faith, believing that the wind exists, and consider just for a moment that God is real and loves you dearly and that He has tried to show you evidence of His hand in your life through goose bump moments?

Waking up in the middle of the night with abuse constantly before me, I lived in utter terror and darkness. Hope was swallowed up, and I could barely breathe. I was treated like an object, used, violated, and tossed around from one person to the next. This darkness occurred for five and a half years of my childhood but haunted me for years after in nightmares, and anytime someone tried to get close to me, I recoiled. I was afraid to sleep at night for fear of waking up screaming and crying from a nightmare of memories that were real. I would have recurring nightmares that my mother would come after me and harm me. This is what she promised me would happen if I told anyone about my experiences. I lived in fear that someone would abduct me out of my bedroom from my window. When my son was six, he was nearly abducted by a couple, and my heart raced in terror that my baby was in the same danger I lived through, and the memories came flooding back. My darkness was reliving the fearful encounters and extreme worry that it would happen again. My darkness as an adult was fear that I would never be enough or that I would be seen as irreparably broken because I was so severely sexually abused. My darkness grew to an unimaginable size—I was diminished to nothing. I was worthless, and I was treated like it was my fault by some people, even after the abuse. My darkness came to a halt after the betrayal of someone I loved dearly and trusted with my life. I came before God and pleaded with Him to break this chain of utter blackness from a lie that had trailed me my whole life since I was very young—that I was worthless, broken, damaged, and unlovable. Thankfully, God finally broke that chain! I had to believe it and embrace that I am lovable and beautiful that God saw everything, and it was not my fault—not anything anyone said over me or did to me was because of me. They acted out of their brokenness. However, the truth is, I am valuable, and I do matter: I am a child of God! A daughter of the King!

If you have experienced the familiarity of being treated so badly that you can hardly breathe, that your very existence is hated, or you have felt underappreciated and demeaned, then you understand what it feels like to have a black cloud hanging over you. Criticism built up over time wears on a person. It takes at least five positive, affirming statements and experiences to counter one negative one. As you can imagine, I had to clear the dresser of my life that became stuffed full overtime, where lies, hurt, and unaffirming truths became stuck in the drawers of my life, and instead, clear through the memories inside, to make space for who I really am: making space for new affirmations and truth. I often have needed to remind myself daily that I am a good enough mom; I am nothing like my biological mother or the men she allowed into my life, or the horrible human trafficking culture; I am nothing like the negativity spoken over me by angry, bitter, jealous, or selfish individuals in my life. I am not broken, damaged goods, and certainly not worthless. On the contrary, *I am valuable. I am a warrior. I am a survivor.* I am an advocate for the underserved; I am a supporter of those who have felt small in their life, who have had no voice like children. I am strong and valuable, worthy of love and belonging, acceptance and support, and God created me for a purpose. These truths became fortified in my mind, heart, and soul, but to strengthen myself and grow into this new mindset, I had to rewire my brain, retrain my thinking, do the hard work of deep trauma therapy, and grieve. I had to embrace who God created me to be and how healthy, supportive people see me, then practice living that out. Through writing down these truths, working through them with support, saying them out loud, then believing them with my heart, soul, and core, and with the power of God, the renewal of my mindset, emotions, past trauma, and current perspective has transpired. It has not been an easy journey. I have shed many tears and thought, "Why do I have to grieve another loss or trauma?" It became so evident to me that God had me in the palm of His hand, that He scooped me up and out of the evil I lived in, and that God had my back the whole time. I just had to learn to attune my thinking, my hearing of His "still small voice," and quiet the noise around me, the lies, the evil forced upon me, and embrace that *I am nothing like those that harmed me*; I am much more! I am a treasure fashioned uniquely by the God of the universe.

Perhaps you can relate. You have had negative experiences, where lies were spoken into and over you, where people: have spoken untruthful things of you, underappreciated you, taken advantage of you, made fun of you, bullied you, physically abused you, emotionally abused you, sexually abused you, gaslighted (sophisticated manipulation) you, and trampled your identity. I'm here to tell you that you can rise up from the darkness and find purpose and hope. God sees you, and you are not alone or hopeless. Sometimes when we have heard our thoughts repeat what others have said, like a movie reel stuck on replay, we forget that we can stop the movie and choose not to listen and believe the lies. We can adapt the script and transform the movie of our lives. Rewrite the narrative from our perspective but this time with truth. It takes a warrior, a strong-hearted, grit-driven individual, to dust off their feet, wash off the blood and dirt and grime, and say, "No more! I deserve better! I'm tired of hearing and experiencing this same cruelty and feeling bad about myself! I am a survivor, not a victim anymore. I am strong and will figure out the next step."

Perhaps consider a few brave steps to start with that may include: opening your awareness, having the motivation to walk the path of healing, and starting to see value in yourself. With the help of mentors, dear friends, trauma therapists, and my faith, over time, I rebuilt my identity, this time not defined by the trauma but having risen up out of the trauma—that is how I am able to share this story with you. Every word I share helps dispel the darkness; because no enemy can stand against God, and no more unhealthy people will be allowed in my life. I learned to set boundaries. When hurts come up, I see them differently, create space for the individual, and process the grief or trauma, while reminding myself of my value, worth, and purpose in pain. I deal with hardships, trauma, and difficulties on a level that integrates my resilience, my ability to bounce back, have wholesome perspective taking, and my strength to press on. I continue to share and use the pain as a springboard for empathy, understanding, and healing when helping others or connecting with others. I have learned to separate what is my issue and what is the other person's. I have learned to reparent myself and give myself grace when I make mistakes. I encourage you to pause here and take a few slow, deep breaths. Acknowledge that you, too, have the potential, and capacity to heal, that you are valuable. If this feels unfamiliar or uncomfortable, just accept that. It is okay to be where you are on this journey. No pressure that you should be anywhere else. Awareness begins with living in the moment and allowing your senses, your mind, and your heart to align to show you the truth of where you are and where you want to go. I believe in you. I have struggled, but it is in the struggle that rebirth and growth transpire. It is a beautiful messiness that God can impact, and we can learn to be reshaped and to shape our identities and worth.

The key is this: that moment when you say—Wait! Enough is enough!—that is your *illuminating moment. That glimmer of light, of hope, spreads across your life.* When I realized I loved the difficult people I encountered in my life to the best of my ability and that

I learned through therapy that my feelings and struggles from the grief and loss were normal, I had in that moment become freed from them. I was accepting what is truth, and as it is said, the truth will set you free! I literally felt this weight taken from my shoulders—"it's not me." *Releasing the lies of the past can enable you to become who you truly are meant to be.* I can really see beauty in nature and embrace things with gratitude and joy. I can see people with their good and bad qualities and accept them, not pause as I would hold my breath in fear of getting hurt in the past or that I could not trust people. I could taste new flavors and savor them differently. I did not have to starve or just get by. I could change my wardrobe and wear clothes that flattered me, and I felt more confident in myself without fear of someone taking advantage of me or being criticized for what I wore or my body type. I could speak bolder, with love and kindness, but take more initiative with confidence, and be firm if necessary, without guilt, fear of retaliation, or worry.

I gave myself permission to say no. I did not have to quiet myself because I am a woman or because that is what my experience taught me but that I could be equal with others, and treat others with dignity and respect, how I hope to be treated. I still need to remind myself it is okay to assert myself. Even in our current culture, I need to be assertive and confident, but at the same time, I still utilize my self-awareness gauge, as I am always learning new ways of being and thinking. However, this time it is from a lens of self-respect, value, and acceptance of who I am. Despite the pain from my past, I now walk with purpose, intention, and joy, creating new memories with my children, living vicariously through them, capturing them in moments and photographs, and relishing in their expressions, innocence, joy, and idiosyncrasies. When I did not grow up with a normal childhood, with a baby book, or playing outside, I found through looking through my children's eyes, or other children, this new sense of freedom, imagination, unrequited spontaneous joy, and curious exploration that everything is new for the first time! One mantra I live by is: living in carpe diem—seizing each moment, breathing it in, and learning how to thrive more each day.

You, too, can come to this posture of peace, acceptance, self-awareness, and joy. I have done it, and so have others. I believe in you that you can too. Find that light inside you, the one that tells you that you are worth it, that helps you get up in the morning, that reminds you today is worth living. Then, believe in that spark, the glimmer of hope, and start walking. You do not have to have all the answers. Just keep breathing and walk.

There is a powerful piece of Scripture that enlightens all of what we have unearthed in this chapter. Second Samuel 22:29–36 (excerpts) states,

> For You, O Lord, are my lamp; The Lord illuminates and dispels my darkness. As for God…He is a shield to all those who take refuge and trust in Him. For who is God, besides the Lord? And who is a rock, besides our God? God is my strong fortress; He sets the blameless in His way. He makes my feet like the doe's feet [firm and swift]; He sets me [secure and confident] on my high places. You have also given me the shield of Your salvation, and your help and gentleness make me great.[29]

These beautiful words speak to the truth that we will each encounter darkness, but God's lamp will dispel or scatter the darkness! *Swoosh*! It is gone! How powerful is that comforting thought! In the midst of your journey—whatever you may label as your darkness, whether addiction, spending, pride, self-sabotage, beating yourself up, suicidal thoughts or self-harm, giving up, or harm done to you that caused enormous pain, grief, trauma, and fear…*nothing is too much for God's lamp to illuminate*. God desires to quench the chains the darkness has caused. He longs to draw you closer to Him and scatter the darkness, and renew the spark in you. An important distinction is this: *you are not the darkness, or your addictions, or choices,*

---

[29] Second Samuel 22:29–36 (Amplified).

or the actions done to you—you are more than that. Jesus died to show you what love is, and He accepts you just the way you are. He also loves you so much. He doesn't want to leave you in your hurting state. He showed Himself to me in powerful ways and continues to keep my lamp burning. I am more than how I was treated and misguided steps along the way—that is what the voice of mercy and grace is.

Moment of reflection

I invite you to take a moment to write down a few thoughts or feelings that surfaced for you, something you gained or learned from this chapter. I also invite you to repeat to yourself. I am not defined by _____________. You fill in the blank. Instead, I am defined by _____________. Then take a moment to offer yourself grace at this moment. This may look like saying to yourself, "I am proud of you for having the courage to _____________." Maybe you feel courageous for reading this book and getting this far. Maybe you feel brave that you are considering seeing yourself in a new light. Lastly, I invite you to take a walk or do something that would be honoring to yourself. It could be a small gesture or a big one. Honor yourself for the battles you have endured in your life.

CHAPTER 6

Miraculous Meaning

Shame resilience is key to embracing our vulnerability.[30]
—Dr. Brene Brown

Shame resilience…the ability to practice authenticity when we
experience shame, to move through the experience without
sacrificing our values, and to come out on the other side of
the shame experience with more courage, compassion, and
connection than we had going into it. Shame resilience is about
moving from shame to empathy—the real antidote to shame.[31]
—Dr. Brene Brown

As we journey through the second half of this book, I encourage
you to stay present and mindful of what you can do to take care of
yourself. I began writing this while sitting in quarantine from the
COVID-19 virus in 2020–2022 and even after the peak season of
the pandemic. Little did any of us know that this virus would shut
down the planet and impact our world on such a grand scale. My
heart has gone out to families, children, older adults, and homeless
persons that have been so impacted by the pandemic. Many lives lost

---

[30] Dr. Brene Brown, *Daring Greatly: How the Courage to Be Vulnerable Transforms the Way we Live, Love, Parent, and Lead* (England: Penguin Books, 2012), 61.

[31] Dr. Brene Brown, *Daring Greatly: How the Courage to Be Vulnerable Transforms the Way we Live, Love, Parent, and Lead* (England: Penguin Books, 2012), 74.

and so much uncertainty. How can we find meaning in the midst of monumental moments of suffering in our lives? How do you find purpose in a family that takes out their anger on their children or spouse in violence? Have you ever felt that there was no point in this job, marriage, or your life? You are not alone. In this passage, we will walk together through the arduous journey of piecing together meaning in the midst of pain.

As I reflect on how I came to create meaning in my story and all the trauma I endured, I can honestly say that it was a process that unfolded moment by moment, and chapter by chapter, and through understanding "shame resilience"[32] and how to unpack my story, be more honest and vulnerable in sharing, and pausing before believing the shame and lies spoken over me. I often reflected on memories and would recall new information and see a new perspective as I grew into the person I am today. In the beginning, I had to sift through various emotions tied to memories and try to make sense of that first before journeying to the next step of healing, accepting grief and loss of what did and did not occur, and eventually reaching a place of gratitude, recognizing God's hand in each moment, and my strength to persevere. At times, I would see the memories of my story as if others around me were harmed, but not me. In other instances, I would see from a shocking point of view that I could not believe I had survived so much; it's a miracle I survived, and I am alive! I had survived near-death experiences. Noticing when unnecessary shame and guilt were intruding upon my life was key to being able to free myself from the triggers that chained me at times. Increasing my awareness of when these messages would come into my mind, and speaking truth to them, were essential. I would reach out for support when I would feel stuck, knowing that something was not true, but my body and emotions felt unworthy. I then moved to a state of self-compassion and worth, where I could say no to the shame, and there I began to see more resilience surface. This beautiful moment really made it

---

[32] Dr. Brene Brown, *Daring Greatly: How the Courage to Be Vulnerable Transforms the Way we Live, Love, Parent, and Lead* (England: Penguin Books, 2012), 74–75.

worth going through the difficulties and struggles. There really is a light at the end of the tunnel. Only the light is another chapter, not the end, to help with endurance and feeding hope.

On some occasions earlier in my life, I had survivor's guilt. "Why did I survive and others did not (when I was stuck in human trafficking)? What is the point of me being here after such horrific times? Other times, I was sad and cried often, especially at times when I felt alone and wondered why no one was looking for me or protecting me (such as when I was in the hotel rooms, desperately wanting to escape). I would cry wishing I had someone to go to, who I could rely on, who was consistent, when I felt sad, scared, or needed comfort. At times, I felt angry for all the injustice and abuse, for the stress, and for having to go through difficult times after difficult times. As a young child, I often felt invisible, like no one cared, and instead went about their own business, fulfilling their own interests. Other times, I felt alone, wishing I had a sister or someone close I could confide in and trust. We all go through difficult seasons, and most individuals experience some form of trauma or loss in their life. Sometimes it may feel overwhelming and defeating. The fact that you are here reading this shows that you have made it this far, and clearly, you have a purpose.

As I grew older and met people with different stories of surviving trauma, loss, and negative foster care experiences, I became inspired and began to form a narrative of my own. I learned from others and began to piece together moments of meaning and positive reframes of the negative, evil experiences I endured. I was not alone because others had been there. I often would "try on" their strength to endure difficult times when I felt life was too much. I believed it was possible to persevere because God had shown me in the Bible and the amazing lives of great people making a difference in the world. Some were friends, colleagues, teachers, mentors, choir directors, prayer warriors, and some were family. I have learned to grow a tribe of trustworthy people and rebuild it when needed. Through it all, I realized God's hand was in my life from day one. Though I did not know him when I was a child, and I did not see Him with my eyes, I learned to walk by faith, not by sight.

Even as I've been writing this book, I experienced another near-death experience. This time, it was acute appendicitis. I was so accustomed to pain, physical and emotional, that I almost did not go to urgent care and subsequently the ER. It was by God's hand, and trusting that my body was telling me something was not right, as I was in the later stages of the medical emergency, and it had radiated to all my abdominal area, I listened, and God's hand through each nurse and doctor led me to receive emergency surgery. In fact, God protected my mind and heart right up to and during the procedure because I was not aware of how severe it was. I had prepared my kids for any possible emergency, and here it was. I prayed and told God I trusted Him to guide every step and lean only on Him. As I woke up from the general anesthesia, the surgeon came out and said, "Thank goodness you came in. We almost lost you. I got your appendix out just in time." I was in utter shock. Gratitude filled my being, bubbling up and pouring out uncontrollably. I told every doctor or nurse, "Thank you for all you do!" I saw the look in family's and friend's eyes that day and suddenly understood—they thought they were going to lose me, even my children. Friends, neighbors, and family stepped in and brought food, support, and prayers. I was speechless. Everything happened so quickly. I hugged my children so tightly and thanked them for being so brave and how sorry I was to scare them. I reassured them, "God had me the whole time, and He had you too." People stepped in to provide comfort and support to my teenagers. Light shone so brightly, and the light illuminated the deeper, miraculous meaning of my life in the midst of darkness. Suddenly, an illumination—I had survived again! I had a renewed humility and purpose. I am finishing this book as I am healing from this major surgery.

The biggest miracle for me in my life has been witnessing God's hand imprinted on my life, as evidenced in the golden thread, His hand, woven throughout my life from all the people He placed in my life that have touched my life and then seeing and understanding how God has redeemed my life, purpose, and identity through these powerful experiences. I lost sight of who I was because I was not initially modeled love, nurture, patience, grace, and protection, especially in my earlier childhood. I began to seek out mentors and took on traits that fit as I was slowly piecing myself together. As it turns out, I am funny, adventurous, outdoorsy, creative, strong, resilient, empathic, an advocate for others, and much more. Considering all that I survived, I was grateful and humbled that I could more fully see who I really am and was touched by the hand of God and His golden threads throughout my life.

Moments of reflection

As you look at your life, think of when you first began to see glimmers of who you are, how you came to realize that, and what helped you overcome obstacles in your life. Was it a caring grandparent, or friend down the street, or the song you heard on the radio?

If you still are piecing yourself and life together, that is okay. We are all in it for the ride, and the right wave will come. You will feel an illumination of hope and purpose. Things will begin to click, and you will know that you are here for a reason. You went through what you lived through for a purpose. You are at the wheel and can decide where you want to steer next; however, not without strife, challenges, and obstacles. These seasons of pain are there to shape us, create us, grow us, and frame us into stronger, braver, wiser person. It starts with believing in what is unseen, looking beyond the circumstance, and embracing breathless moments of joy, beauty, triumph, tears, growth, and progress. Creating miraculous meaning can come from a tribe, or community, faith, and/or self-actualization, determination, and acceptance. Just as the serenity prayer posits: "to accept the things I cannot change, courage to change the things I can, and wisdom to know the difference…"

I often thought that if I could make amends or forgive and build a bridge with any person with whom there was a misunderstanding or pain, then I would feel peace. Well, in my experience, that type of experience is rare; a true gem if there is mutual reconciliation. Many times, others are not in a place of having done their own work of healing, or even fully enough, and their wounds can wound others.

However, God reconciled the broken pieces of the stained-glass window in my life and has created something far more beautiful, breathtaking, and awe-inspiring. But to tap into that restoration project and find peace and wholeness is a choice. It takes great strength and bravery. Peace in God always exists. But research shows that what you focus your mind and thoughts on is what you begin to embody. If we constantly think about the people that hurt us, others' mistakes or shortcomings, or our own, or the relationships that became broken, we can never move on. Sometimes grieving them, letting them go, and surrendering them to God is the only thing you can do to find healing. This involves accepting that you are only responsible and capable of controlling yourself. If you need to shift things inside you and how you are, that requires great courage. Wisdom knows which pieces are movable and which are immovable in yourself and in relationships. Finding peace and purpose during the messiness and chaos in the world is truly a gift of creating miraculous meaning. Through each hill and valley, you may need to reevaluate things and find new meaning amid journeying to find truth while searching for a break between the forest and the trees. Life can get complicated! Can we all agree? Sometimes messiness and chaos seem purposeless, frustrating, or heartbreaking. Will this ever end? You are just trying to keep your head above water; this can seem like a heavy burden and weighty. Needing a respite, a refreshing deep breath, rest, relaxation, and peace—whatever it is that you need, pay attention to it.

Moment of reflection

You are worthy of belonging, you matter, you are a fighter, and you've come this far. Just waking up and taking a deep breath of air and releasing it—a miraculous meaningful miracle. And I am so incredibly grateful you are present and reading this. You are a miracle.

My hope is that you can begin this passage of time by creating meaning with your story. Recognizing through creating a vision board of images that speak to you, a photography collage, traveling to new and inspiring places, eating delicious foods, savoring moments of laughter and good times with special people, and creating meaningful moments, that you can rebuild, and refill the dresser drawers of your life with newly revived memories and pieces of you. This entails going through each drawer one at a time, taking out each piece of memory, and deciding if it will add to your life or not. Then make space for new meaningful things to fill the drawers of your life. My belief is that God created us each with His miraculous imprint, and He wanted to knit us together to have deeper relationships with Him and others. We are wired for connection and meaning. What can you do today to begin your journey or write the next chapter of creating miraculous meaning in your own life? You are created for a purpose. Trust the process of growth, understanding, and changes that can help bring positive transformation. May hope, meaning, and purpose increase within you!

In his newly released book *Created to Dream: The 6 Phases God Uses to Grow Your Faith*, Rick Warren speaks of God offering second chances to individuals with the intention of creating newness and meaning, often through dreams.[33] "What he calls you to do, he will enable you to do—in his timing and his way...never give up on the dreams God created you to dream. He will never give up on you."[34] In other words, there is a purpose that is greater than the pain and suffering you have endured or witnessed others endure; there is a greater purpose beyond your pain. I recognized in my own life that God began planting seeds of compassion for others: for the ostracized, lonely, hurting, left out, marginalized, and those dealing with scarcity, fear, or sadness. Rather than feeling stuck in fear, I felt prompted to listen to others share their stories and provide support and care. God planted a dream in me long before the evil that occurred to me in my life. The difference is God decided to use the hypervigilance and insightfulness that I gained through stretching my senses beyond their limits to carefully and intuitively sit with

---

[33] Rick Warren, *Created to Dream: The 6 Phases God Uses to Grow Your Faith* (Michigan: Zondervan Books, 2023), 114–115.

[34] Rick Warren, *Created to Dream: the 6 Phases God Uses to Grow Your Faith* (Michigan: Zondervan Books, 2023), 115.

others in their pain and provide strength and encouragement for healing.

Moment of reflection

You are a warrior in the making. You are learning to trust what you have seen, felt, and experienced as tools to understand others and bring meaning to your story and the story of others. This world needs you and your experiences. Hope, kindness, and compassion are rare treasures that are essential for survival and eventually for thriving. There is miraculous meaning in the person you are today. Imagine for a moment what it would look like to allow yourself to dream; let your thoughts carry you to something that you have always wanted to do, create, support, advocate, build bridges, and pour into others... The possibilities are endless. What if you believed that that dream was already in you before everything that occurred in your life took place? What if you believed you already had it in you to succeed, to heal, to at last find what you have been looking for that is truly lasting? What if you believed you could? What if you let go of what was missing in your past, what was holding you back, and you stepped forward, believing it is possible? You were born for a miraculous miracle.

CHAPTER 7

Realizations of Redemption

Loving myself, and seeing that I am truly loveable, has
been one of the most arduous battles of my life. Once I
have embraced that I am worthy of love, and in fact am
lovable, I have begun to see a glimmer of what redemption
is about—seeing myself through the eyes of God.

—Dr. Tiffany Modica

Welcome back, beloved warriors. One of the biggest growth passages
I have ever encountered is realizing redemption in my life! These are
the earth-shaking, life-altering, majestic moments that leave you in
utter awe. You are shocked, crying tears of joy, so much so that you
lose your ability to speak! These were the moments when I began
to put the biggest puzzle pieces together in my life in a way that
made sense, brought purpose and meaning, sparked illumination,
and brought life-giving realizations to fuller awareness. Redemption
is regaining back what was lost and more. I longed to be rescued
from the terror of my tender years. Redemption scooped me up and
preserved parts of me that enabled me to survive such evil, neglect,
and loneliness.

First, let us break down what I mean by "redemption." According
to the *Oxford Learner's Dictionary* online, redemption is defined as
"the act of saving or state of being saved from the power of evil, the

act of redeeming."[35] If you have ever encountered a loss of a loved one, abuse, trauma, a house break-in, violence, job loss, or threats to your life, the idea of being saved from evil might sound like a miracle or a redemptive experience. With the idea of redemption, your life was saved, or your loved one was spared. What if you endured horrific trauma and were not saved? How would you realize redemption? Is there purpose in pain? Can you rise from the ashes of bitter despair, utter sadness, or even a life shift from a miscarriage, a spouse cheating, a best friend's betrayal, or an unexpected car accident and major physical injuries?

This chapter will dive into how to remove either rose-colored glasses or negatively colored shades on your eyes to unveil something beautiful, maybe unexpected, and unimaginable beyond all you could ever ask or think or imagine. Can you see the forest through the trees? The light at the end of the tunnel? Or do you feel like your grave is being dug, that the four walls you live inside are closing in on you? Is hope seeming to be squeezed out by despair, a possibility being flattened by drowning sadness, or deep core loss overwhelming you like a tsunami? You are not alone. Everyone goes through at least one of these experiences. Your perspective and your shade of vision do influence how you look at what has happened to you and your outlook on life.

Growing up in poverty, in fear, and without comfort, this was normal for me—I did not see what life was like outside the run-down motel, living in a car, or on the scary streets we navigated. I had never experienced what it was like to run, jump, and play in the sunshine with friends without worries, nor was I acquainted with creating stories and exploring nature. Instead, I was left in a constant state of fight, flight, or freeze. My life was small, and I felt trapped. I felt alone, and my basic needs of safety, love, belonging, and food were not met. My lens toward the world became precarious, doubtful, skeptical, fearful, and especially without rose-colored glasses.

---

[35] Oxford Learners Dictionary. (Online: Oxford University Press, 2023) "redemption," https://www.oxfordlearnersdictionaries.com/us/definition/english/redemption?q=redemption, www.oxfordlearnersdictionary.com.

I saw things in stereo live, in action, surviving each moment. I so wanted to change the channel or turn the volume down or off, but I had no other alternative. In that, I had very limited space to grow and expand my vision. I first needed to be removed from the awful upbringing to a place of safety, warmth, and nurturance, where my basic needs began to be met. I was eventually discovered "by accident," as I recalled, by police in a parked car in front of a motel. I was later put in foster care. After that, I was finally fed three meals a day, given vaccinations for the first time at seven and a half, wore clothes besides the one outfit I owned, and attended school for the first time. I could not read or write and understand math concepts. While school kids were around me and played, I sat and watched everyone. I did not know how to be a kid and play without fear. I was a foreigner in a strange land. Everything was so new and daunting.

Fast forward to age thirty. I was sitting in a trauma therapy session, and my therapist helped make the first connection that I had a caring foster mother with whom I talked differently about and appeared to show enough love, nurture, care toward me, and shared experiences while creating a safe environment for me to grow. She would understand my struggles and help me with reading and schoolwork. She believed in me and taught me never to give up. She would let me play outside. I grew to love nature. I joined Brownies and Girl Scouts, and she helped me collect patches, go camping, cook, and explore. I had never tapped into my imagination before. Additionally, I joined the swim team, where I medaled. I felt confident and joy that I could do something on my own. She supported each step of new experiences and the growing pains of feeling behind and "not smart enough." She showed me grace when I was hard on myself. If it was not for these beginning experiences, I would not know how to parent my children or know I love to be outside in nature, swim, connect with my love for singing, and have my faith in God established. She took me to church, where I sang and performed musicals. I had a song in my heart and joy in my spirit as a young child—a newfound experience for me. She took me to Royal Family Kids Camp (RFKC), where I came to know about God and accept Him into my heart. I was invited into God's family, where I could feel loved and accepted. I was thrilled! It was there where I began connecting to others, and I felt understood in what it was like to be in foster care. I was in the company of others who had experienced abuse, trauma, and neglect, and I found redemption in being a part of this supportive community and a part of God's family. Little did they know, RFKC was ahead of their time in the early '90s, creating environments to share God's love but also foster resilience in foster children. These experiences imprinted on my life, and a new narrative was being penned, another realization of redemption. I was not alone. I was seen. I was valuable.

One step further, God continued to weave His golden threads of healing and redemption through various people I met through the years. One person helped shed light and meaning, and this helped me to realize where God had redeemed my story. For instance, I became acutely aware that God had scooped me out of the abuse. It was not by accident that I was found—it was purposeful! God willed it to happen to show me my value and provide a miracle. This miracle, I discovered later, was so I could sit with others in their pain, be acquainted with feeling trapped and powerless, and provide therapeutic support and healing. Then a little over a year later, after I was put in foster care, I met my foster mom, Jean, who showered me with love and care even though she could be rough around the edges at times. She had lived a hard life and had many health issues but constantly sacrificed herself for me and other foster children. I felt safe with her. I shared with her one piece of my abuse story, and she believed me. This taught me that I could find safe people to trust. She shaped me to be a person of perseverance, even when life became arduous.

God provided other periods of healing through relationships with others through friendships in school and college, mentors, other foster children, teachers, therapists, and colleagues. My internal strength grew through each encounter, confirming that I was on the path I was called to go. My adoptive parents provided for my needs in ways I had not encountered in my earlier childhood experiences while on the streets in poverty. They believed in me and demonstrated how to be giving, which came so easily to me once I learned this essential value. They gave me experiences that expanded my love of the arts and singing, musicals, seeing live music including symphonies and bands, world traveling and choir tours, appreciation for quality music, and helped support my love of music, writing, helping others, and raising my kids. In my previous relationships, even with the pain embedded, I was able to separate the good from the bad and take in words such as, "You are the strongest and most courageous person I know." I connected with biological cousins in the Pacific Northwest after my undergraduate degree, who are near and dear to my heart now, and they accepted me with open arms, with heart-warming strength and encouraging words, and the reminder that "We adopted you back into our family." My biological aunt and uncle provided a home for me while in foster care and extended support after I was adopted, which was invaluable. I had become a part of other families and communities now, even since I was little when I did not have a safe place to call home. I am truly grateful for these redemptive moments and people that have shaped, strengthened, and touched my heart and life. Now I can hold onto people better than before—another piece of redemptive healing.

Life did not follow a sequential path that was suddenly easy once I was removed from the severe abuse of my earlier childhood. I was faced with many battles, many times which felt so overwhelming I would feel flooded emotionally. Crying was where I would go often. I would listen to music that spoke to me and try to hold onto the good that had come into my life, hold onto God's truth, or the people that spoke to my heart and soul. However, at times, I struggled so much due to severe attachment trauma and inconsistent caregivers in my life that I felt swallowed up by the pain, nightmares, body memories of abuse, and felt emotionally stuck and alone. I could not hold onto people long enough to feel emotionally safe and nurtured. My foster mom was pivotal in my life, but I was taken away from her due to unfounded complaints made against her. She was going to adopt me. I was devastated. I had been adopted once previously, and the adoption failed due to abuse, and I was put back in the system. I was tossed around, even in foster care, feeling retraumatized.

I needed stability. I would file away the good experiences, but I would dissociate when the bad would occur or feel flooded by the previous trauma. I needed a safer, consistent holding environment. Much like a crying child needs to be held and soothed by their parent—I did not have enough of those experiences. I often was ignored or expected to just be a good child. This emotional neglect added insult to injury and created layers of trauma through the years. I went from the frying pan back into the fire repeatedly. Throughout my entire life, I can say that I have endured a great deal of trauma: betrayal, abandonment, abuse on all levels, manipulation, gaslighting, bullying, being used and objectified, physical and emotional neglect, violence, witnessing violence, being drugged, assaulted, and surviving five near-death experiences (two medical related, one at birth, and one in my adult years; three due to severe abuse). Despite these horrific experiences, which could easily become roadblocks, I have pressed on and endured by believing in something greater than my circumstances. Not giving power to the abusers but redefining my identity after each encounter. This is the definition of resilience, bouncing back despite unforeseen circumstances, against all odds, and miraculous redemption. One percent of foster youth graduate with a college degree. In 2019, I graduated with my doctorate in clinical psychology. I cried at my graduation. I could not believe I made it this far. Again, a defining moment and realization of redemption.

In my life, God brought different people throughout different seasons to reflect God's heart of compassion and love, bringing redemptive meaning to my story, reminding me of my value and purpose for surviving all I endured. Each piece happened for a reason, and I was not by accident. You are not by accident. Your experiences are a piece of your story, but not who you are. Your story is being redeemed one page at a time. I would have to remind myself of that very thing—because it is easy to get caught up in circumstances as time goes by and wonder why God is allowing this or that. I reminded myself that we live in a fallen world where there is brokenness and woundedness all around us. Wounded people wound others. Remembering to keep a bigger picture, a wider perspective, enables us to view things in the context of our whole story. Bit by bit, my story's pieces fit together.

The broken pieces of my past became remolded into a beautiful masterpiece as I began to believe and claim God's redemption, calling me by name and solidifying that I belong to Him. My identity shifted in a positive direction, becoming shaped by my strength, bravery, and perseverance through awful experiences. Additionally, I became shaped by those that spoke truth through their genuine care and authenticity, and strength into me, as they believed in me. This conglomeration of experiences, emotions, growth, and adventures was beautifully handcrafted together and uniquely shaped. I am truly grateful and humbled. These refining experiences became evidence that the golden threads of God's redemption were in my life and that these impactful experiences created deep meaning that began spotlighting aspects of my character, personality, values and virtues, passion, and purpose in an illuminated fashion.

Moment of reflection

I want to encourage you to pause right now. Take out a journal or paper and list the qualities that you have, and begin to point them back to moments when you experienced hope, bridges, indications that you were a warrior, light shining in the darkness, and where there is meaning coming out of situations. Next, I encourage you to write down moments when you felt redeemed, such as when someone stepped in to offer kindness, hope, love, care, or rescue you. These are moments of redemption—both big and small. Then walk away, come back later and review the list, and add to it if anything else comes to mind.

Realizations of redemption come when we open our minds and hearts to ourselves, our stories, and the possibility of rebuilding, hope, restoration, renewal, and healing. For me, this looked like the hand of God reaching into my life in unexpected ways, like in the mentors and figures or music and verses that melted into the deep recesses of my heart and spirit. The core of me was stronger, more resolute, and grounded than I ever even realized. I can now say that

I look back and see I am who I am because of the truth I pulled out of the culmination of experiences I have encountered and the perseverance I have that keeps me moving forward. But I can't forget that my value is held in the loving arms of God, where my true identity is as a child of God. No circumstance or situation can detract from that beloved truth. We will next journey into the Holding Place. Be well, beloved readers.

CHAPTER 8

Roadblocks and Holding Place

John Bowlby, the Father of Attachment, researched and
wrote about the importance of attachment figures, in finding
safety and security in a "safe base," knowing that your
needs will be met, and you will be seen and valued.[36]

Imagine preparing for a journey, packing food, clothing, books, and
seasonal items and feeling excited and ready for a new adventure.
With preparations to embark set, you fully organize your vehicle with
your essentials, back out of the car, and head out on your way. Then
suddenly, unbeknownst to you, not even a quarter way on your journey, your car begins to veer dramatically in different directions, and
"pop!" the tire explodes! You come to a screeching halt. You have hit
a roadblock. You were intentional in your preparation, excited for the
journey, and then life hit you. Does this sound familiar to you? Can
you identify with the feelings of stress, worry, or panic? You receive
an unexpected medical diagnosis, cancer, severe pain, job loss, infer-
tility, loss of a child or spouse or sibling, unemployment, or a natural
disaster that takes your home. These roadblocks feel discouraging,
unexpected, fuel fear, helplessness, hopelessness, despair, weariness,

---

[36] John Bowlby. *A Secure Base: Parent-Child Attachment and Healthy Human
Development* (London: Routledge, 1988), 123.

and you feel stuck. You were on a path. Things were going well… until this roadblock hit you right to the core. What do I do now?

How do you typically deal with sudden life changes and challenges? Do you feel overwhelmed and want to quit? Do you want to continue and press on? Do you feel like you are spinning and confused? All these are normal responses to life's challenges or sudden trauma that you may encounter. During my earlier childhood roller coaster journey, I found myself feeling stuck often. I would vacillate between feeling fearful and frozen, feeling terrorized and alone, withdrawing and feeling helpless, thinking I could control the situation and find a way out, or believing in faith beyond myself that Someone could help me or save me. Pastor Rick Warren recently said in his newly published book, *Created to Dream* (2023, p95), "The situation may be out of your control, but it is not out of God's control. When you face a dead end, don't focus on what you *cannot* do. Focus on what God *can* do." In the clinical therapy work I have done, when clients have come to the point of an impasse, I often use a technique of forward-thinking where I ask them, "What can you do?" This is an approach called Acceptance Commitment Therapy (ACT), where therapists model methods of thinking more flexibly, accepting situations that are out of their control, and making future plans. See, we often feel stuck in the emotion that is triggered by the trauma—I lost this promotion; therefore, I feel like a failure. Fear underlying the negative belief, and the accompanying belief is, "I am stuck, feel immobile, and helpless."

As a young child, my brain, emotions, and identity were still developing, so I was unable to fully understand everything that was happening to me and around me. Part of my setbacks were related to the toxic environment that surrounded me. I longed to play and be a normal kid, have the freedom to explore and be creative, eat food and fun snacks, participate in art and sports, and play with other kids, but the adults in my environment were more concerned about their agenda, training me to be compliant for sex trafficking than to allow me to develop as a child, and meet my needs in healthy ways. My other roadblocks were my limited coping and the resources available to me. I was put in an environment and raised by a biological parent who was limited due to her mental illness and selfish choices. Therefore, I did not have a healthy understanding of what was safe and okay for adults and what was not.

I needed guidance, someone to say, "This is how you brush your teeth or take a bath…this adult was not supposed to handle you this way. A loving parent would make sure you have three meals a day, attend school, see a doctor, and not force you to comply with abusive and coercive acts for money, power, and control over you. You are worth more than this. You are a beautiful child, a daughter of the King. This is not your fault." Additionally, a significant roadblock for me was that I was not mirrored for who I am. As a child, there is an innate need to have a safe and secure base with a parent, a resting place of security, and who the child is becoming. If the child falls down, the parent ideally reflects back to the child their experience and normalizes their feelings, "Aw, you fell down. You will be okay. Let's wash it off and put some medicine on it and a Band-Aid. It's okay to cry. That scrape on the rock hurt." I can recall my then thirteen-year-old daughter playing in the backyard of her cousin's house, exploring and being creative when she started up a small hill and slipped down, gouging her leg. I saw the whole thing happen. I quickly but calmly came to her aid and sat her down, seeing immediate tears and fear in her eyes. I explained that she would be okay. We could clean and cover it. Upon doing that, she was shaking in fear that there was a lot of blood. For the moment, the bleeding stopped, and I elevated the injury. She was in shock, and I rubbed her arm and gave her a cold drink, and told her she was being so brave and that it was okay to be scared, but her body would heal. As the day went on, she walked, and the wound opened up. At that moment, I could see soft tissue and more fluids leaking and quickly arranged an appointment with urgent care. I brought her air pods to listen to music and remained at her side for comfort as she got her first stitches ever. A surgical nurse from a nearby hospital who had been randomly selected to cover a shift at urgent care had been there that day, and flawlessly cleaned, prepped, and provided seven surgical stitches for my daughter, plus an antibiotic to prevent infection. I continually provided words of comfort, gentle caressing and hugs, soothing music, and reminders of how brave and strong she was, and let her know God was looking out for her to send her such an overqualified nurse to help her leg heal and deliver her from any further infection.

Despite this unfortunate situation, I found it amazing how God showed up in the midst and with supportive family around too. Even though I did not grow up initially with an attentive and attuned, nurturing mother, something kicked in—it was resilience and a faith belief that God would guide the process even though I did not have a template to work from fully. As I look back, I realize that my foster mom, Jean, was my first model of care and nurture, as she sat with me when I cried and struggled at age seven and eight years old when I could not read, or when I had pneumonia, and she sat with me all night to help me break my fever. Sometimes I look back and feel sad about what I missed, but then I realize the beauty of God showing up in amazing and awestruck ways to remind us of our value and guide us to resemble His love. In the book *Created to Dream*, Rick Warren states, "Only God can give life to the dead. Only God can create something out of nothing. That's the definition of a miracle...He can make a way where there is no way" (2023, p. 95).[37] Luke 18:27 from the Bible states, "What is impossible with man is possible with God."[38] Having faith in God, remembering to hold onto Hope in His promises, and believing that He will come through, are lessons that I have learned throughout my life to help carry me through life's roadblocks and hang-ups.

During the peak of the COVID-19 pandemic, I was unemployed right after completing my doctorate. I felt so depleted and disappointed and filled with confusion. After over a year of unemployment and applying to forty jobs, God opened a door. Even when I was asked to interview, I was not convinced I would be chosen as the right fit due to carrying self-doubt from numerous rejections that year. Even as I am writing this, I am facing new obstacles. Due to some recent and past health issues, including COVID-19 three times

---

[37] Rick Warren, *Created to Dream: the 6 Phases God Uses to Grow Your Faith* (Michigan: Zondervan Books, 2023), 95.

[38] Luke 18:27 (NIV).

this year, plus some chronic health issues, I am trying to work past a roadblock. Feeling the waves of shock, defeat, weariness, disbelief, confusion, and sadness, I have felt the gamut of emotions. But then, as I allow myself to feel these very real emotions, I remember, "Where God guides, He will provide." He has not taken me this far to suddenly drop me. The pain I have endured in the past as a young child and in the present as an adult is all for a purpose. God not only desires to redeem my pain and reframe it into His purpose but deliver me from it. Just as God used Moses to deliver the Israelites from the Egyptians in the Old Testament, so does God long to deliver you from whatever you are facing. God desires you to see you are valuable, and your pain can be grieved and ultimately transformed for a good purpose. If I knew that one person's life could be changed by me sharing my story of surviving poverty, severe abuse, human trafficking, multiple adoptions, etc., then I have confidence that God knows what He is doing. I survived for a reason: to bring people God's Hope of healing, redemption, and deliverance from their trauma. You, too, deserve this. God has created you for a purpose, and He does not want you to give up or to keep believing any lies spoken over you. The truth is that you are valuable, created for a divine reason, and He wants you to experience His assurance of love and hope and that your life is meaningful.

There is a dynamic practice in Japan where broken pieces of pottery are repaired through *kintsugi*.[39] It is a delicate process of reconnecting the broken pieces using a lacquer, and then they are repainted by the artists through the use of gold or silver that fills the cracks. What is even more fascinating is that these Chawan bowls were considered valuable in their original form but are even more valuable in their mended form. "Kintsugi has a beauty within the imperfection."[40] This practice also brought comfort to family mem-

---

[39] Kato Kyoko, "*Kintsugi:* The Healing Power of Pottery Repair," JapanGov, The Government of Japan, Cabinet Office, August 2020, https://www.gov-online.go.jp/eng/publicity/book/hlj/html/202008/202008_07_en.html.

[40] Kato Kyoko, "*Kintsugi:* The Healing Power of Pottery Repair," JapanGov, The Government of Japan, Cabinet Office, August 2020, https://www.gov-online.go.jp/eng/publicity/book/hlj/html/202008/202008_07_en.html.

bers who lost loved ones from natural disasters such as the Great East Japan Earthquake in March 2011.[41] Creatively integrating broken pieces together can be a soothing and cathartic experience that deepens the sense of purpose and meaning for people.

Moment of reflection

I want you to imagine your life story while taking a moment now to intentionally reflect on what I have shared so far. What might your re-fashioned pottery bowl look like? How would you reshape or redefine the edges, coloring, or even cracks from life's experiences? You have the freedom to choose that your addiction, past mistakes, or past abuse does not have to define your pottery bowl. You have a beautiful story that can be repaired. This starts with recognizing that you are more valuable and beautiful than you may realize.

Holding place

Imagine the idea of being held gently, with only the most loving and comforting embrace imaginable. Safe and secure, knowing that no matter where you go, that holding place is one with which you can return anytime you need. It's consistent, reliable, and real. If this sounds inviting, frightening, daunting, or like you want to avoid—you're not alone. Each person has a different need and view of a holding place. Some people prefer solitude or snuggling with a precious pet. Others need warm human embraces. Others would rather run away because a holding place feels constricting or scary to them. Wherever you are with this—it's okay. But I encourage you to take a leap of faith in this. The truth is, we all need some form of holding place—our sense of self, sense of security, and core strength and peace center on this. For me, I have always had an intrinsic need for hugs and nurturing. I never grew up with it, especially in my

---

41 Kato Kyoko, "*Kintsugi:* The Healing Power of Pottery Repair," JapanGov, The Government of Japan, Cabinet Office, August 2020, https://www.gov-online. go.jp/eng/publicity/book/hlj/html/202008/202008_07_en.html.

formative years, but it was always one of my core needs. I definitely hesitated and would have frozen or run away if there was even a hint of perceived danger. Again, that lens that I had at the beginning sometimes creeps back, and I have to remind myself that I do not live in danger as I did in my earlier childhood. However, God's embrace has always been the most consistent and significant holding place that I can come back to, especially growing up with no protection.

For some, having a holding place and a safe haven is one and the same. I invite you to journey with me on the path of creating a safe space. If you can imagine a new nest of baby birds perched high in the tree. Momma bird circles the nest to make sure the birds are safe and goes hunting for fresh worms to nourish her young. If anything comes near, momma bird becomes instantly protective and swoops low, dive-bombing anything in sight that could jeopardize the lives of her children. She will even risk her life. To the little baby birds, momma bird is their safe haven, as is their nest. What happens if a hawk comes after momma bird or attacks the nest, and suddenly, the baby birds aren't safe? The safe haven becomes shaken. The difference for these birds is that they are used to having a safe haven, and then suddenly, it is not. So what happens if you grow up and your ideal safe haven is actually the source of pain and evil? Do you stop needing a safe haven? Do you forget or have no knowledge that anything else exists? What if your safe haven suddenly changes? In families with divorced parents, children may have grown up in a seemingly safe haven, then find out it is not. Their little, familiar world is suddenly shaken. They do not know who to trust or what will happen. In our world today, with COVID-19, the initial reports of this fast-spreading, unknown virus spread fear and uncertainty faster than the virus itself. That's a picture of what a shaken safe haven looks like.

So how does this differ from a holding place? The safe haven can be more like the environment you grew up in, and you are accustomed to. The holding place could be the actual figures, caregivers, parents, grandparents, foster parents, or siblings that became that comforting place where they could hold you physically or emotionally, and you could always count on them. But most of all—feeling held and safe is key. If you feel held in the nest but not safe, you suddenly see risks, like the nest could fall! Or if you feel safe but lonely, you may lack a place to be held and nurtured. We all have needs, and being held and knowing we are safe, on some level, is essential to survival. Studies suggest that newborn babies in orphanages that are not held and nurtured and grow up without a safe environment fail to thrive. As people with complex traits and needs, the basic needs of safety, security, food, health, and love and belonging are the key to survival. Research supports this over and over.

When sailors embark out to sea and they face torrential weather, they are taught to "hold fast." This means to remain in their place, stay secure, and hold fast to their position. When the storms hit, the waves crash on the sides, the winds rage, and the rain falls in sheets, holding fast is the only option, or you'll fall overboard. Enduring through a challenging environment is the best and the safest strategy. You cannot control your safe haven or your holding place. You cannot change a caregiver that was unavailable to you or abusive, a friend that was neglectful, a boss that took little notice of your impact on the business, or a spouse that was unfaithful. But you can hold fast, persevere, and endure the storm. Part of this includes embracing your resilience. We will journey down this path in the next chapter. But before venturing there, please take a deep breath, know you matter, and you are courageous to journey this far and take a leap of faith. Take care of yourself in this process of growth and awareness. You are an instrument and a bridge for others too but especially yourself.

Finding safety in the right fitting environment, friendships, a therapist, faith and church, and others are key to your healing journey. Allowing space to grieve when you were not held well or treated right is a healing step. Making space for healthier holding places and trusting your intuition when something doesn't feel right with someone is a key step in healing. Furthermore, practicing safe holding with your faith in God or new relationships is important as you practice rebuilding safety in relationships and the resources that you are rebuilding in your toolbox. Language is crucially important, and how you speak to yourself matters. If every time you make a mistake, your inner voice and critic say, "See, I knew you were a failure," over time, you may start to believe it is true. If you begin saying things like, "I know in the past I felt like I was failing, but in this instance, it is different because I made a mistake, but I am growing," this is more of a growth mindset. You are retraining your inner voice to encapsulate an empowering voice of "It is okay to have space to learn from mistakes, and you are growing in these areas!"

Moment of reflection

You have been brave and courageous to read up to this point. I encourage you to pause, breathe, and write down a few things you have learned thus far. I also recommend you take a few slow, deep breaths and say some affirming things to yourself for what you have accomplished, where you are learning and growing, and write one to five gratitude statements. You deserve to hear what you are doing well and what is real and true in your life.

CHAPTER 9

Embracing Resilience

You can get up, you can have a second chance, and God can still use you right where you are in life. Get up and run again. If you are still breathing as you read these words, your story isn't over.[42]
—Greg Laurie

You made it to chapter 9! Congratulations! You persevered. Your willingness and intention to read and be open to growing, sit on tough concepts and ideas, and look at pain and the past from a different stance is truly courageous. I imagine your own story has surfaced too. You are brave to stay the course. There is something special for you in these pages if you endure. You are part of the future, and your story is waiting to be redeemed and shared with others. Even if one person needs to hear your story, it may change the life course of that person. I can think of several encounters where I felt goosebumps and knew in my spirit that this was God speaking and working. God wants to give you goosebump moments if you let Him.

This chapter will take you on a journey of embracing resilience. Many individuals go through life without realizing that they have a great deal of resilience or the potential to develop their resilience more fully. I am one of those individuals that had no awareness of

---

[42] Greg Laurie, *World Changers: How God uses Extraordinary People to Do Extraordinary things* (Michigan: Baker Books, 2020), 20.

what resilience was or that I am a very resilient person. With time, you will come to this realization too.

Have you ever seen the bouncy balls that children collect from toy machines? They have a great deal of high bouncing capability. The idea is that through storms of life, being able to bounce back despite increased difficulties is resilience. We each have different levels of it. Another commonly used term for this is "Grit." It involves robustness, intensity, strength, and perseverance to keep going despite hang-ups. A person with grit has the ability to look at difficulties and see them as opportunities or challenges rather than threats.

I began witnessing semblances of my resilience while working on my doctoral program in psychology as I researched resilience in foster youth. I was sitting with the director of my program, Dr. Girguis, who told me I was one of the most resilient people he had ever met. I thought, "Wow! What a compliment…! What is resilience?" I began to dig into studying resilience in others because I wanted to help others overcome their difficulties, but little did I know and realize that I had it too. I was curious. My story, which I had shared hundreds of times, I shared as facts. But I soon began to piece together the hope behind the neglect and abuse, the bridges created to give me chances when I could have died, the fighter in me that became a warrior and an advocate for the underserved, seeing the light in the midst of darkness, believing in hope that there could be something better that could save me from the awful evil, and embracing meaning from those experiences. I would never harm anyone or become a perpetrator, abuse drugs or alcohol, but rather aim to see people, offer empathy and support, and be a beacon of Hope. I came to stunning realizations of redemption that God had saved me from a horrific childhood that could have resulted in living on the streets permanently, being emancipated out of the foster care system, or worse yet, remaining stuck in human trafficking.

God had always been my safe haven, and He provided different individuals in my life as temporary holding places at times. Embracing my resilience enabled me to be the parent I am today, to help others, see them in their pain, and offer empathy and informed support. I found a purpose in pain that I could share that it is possible to rise up from the ashes and find purpose and hope. I say all this with passion, inspiration, and an emphasis on truth-telling because I believe in my heart and soul that you, too, can persevere through your own journey, no matter where you are in it, no matter how you have learned to cope and find a lit path of hope. You are resilient because you've made it this far. As I continue on my journey, I piece together elements of truth and add to them, refocusing my lens and purpose. Even recently, I have encountered the loss of a dear friend, job loss, and difficult transitions with many challenges. The difference now as compared to other chapters in my life, is that I see the purpose through the pain. This, too, shall pass. I see these hurdles and challenges as a part of God's plan. In every single encounter I have had, God has used me when someone came to me for support or help. You are gifted with specific and special gifts. Your purpose and gifts are meant to be used together.

Part of resilience entails refocusing from your circumstances, your pain, or sources of hurt to looking beyond the pain, growing to see a new perspective like you are standing on the earth, looking down, and seeing people and situations with space in between. It is easy to feel wrapped up in the pain and emotions when it feels overwhelming and is traumatic pain—pain imposed on you. It can be a shock to the system and requires intention, perseverance, and a willingness to grieve the loss and hurt that has happened to you. Refocusing is part of the healing process once you have moved enough through the grief and can see the purpose and meaning behind the circumstances. We can easily become blindsided by situations, and it is a normal human initial response. To step away from and hold the pain while simultaneously being able to see good and hidden nuggets of truth beneath the pain is truly an art form. This was a gift that slowly developed for me.

Another aspect of resilience is remembering to offer yourself grace and understanding as you are growing and learning about yourself, the circumstances and the individuals around you involved in the hurt. In this grace, it is reminding yourself that you matter, your life context matters, and you are valuable, no matter what has happened to you, no matter your mistakes along the way. You are in process. Grace is giving yourself a compassionate word or speaking kindly to yourself when others have misunderstood you and criticized you. Grace is giving yourself extra time and space to figure things out, to sleep a little longer, to provide rest for yourself, and accept your limitations. This can mean setting boundaries for yourself instead of working additional hours to be with your family or get a massage. Grace can mean showing lovingkindness to others, even when they are grumpy, or to yourself when you are being hard on yourself. Sometimes, we can be our worst enemy, taking on the voice of the abuser and turning it on ourselves, almost creating a coalition against us.

In reality, you needed someone to say to you, "This was not your fault. You deserved better." This process of grace, acceptance, self-compassion, and refocusing my words, thoughts, and perspective took time. Even if you do not necessarily believe the negative messages to be true, if you hear enough, they start to become the loudest voice, and you begin responding to them as if they are true. Refocusing and leaning into grace is saying, "Enough! I claim this noise no longer has power over me. I deserve to be treated as a worthy human being with respect and dignity. I do not have to take the abuse anymore, and I never deserved it in the first place! I deserve to have freedom and peace, and rebuild my life and reconstruct my identity!" Resilience is an internal process that involves reconnecting with yourself in a new, empowered, and compassionate manner that no longer allows toxicity to invade your life again. It creates a buffer.

How do I embrace my resilience? First, I had to begin taking a bird's eye perspective of my life and experiences and begin to accept what I have overcome. I have endured severe abuse and neglect, a lack of early childhood education, lacking friendships and early socialization skills, a safe base, and basic needs that were not met (food, shelter, healthcare including dental care and vaccinations, education), and a lack of safety and security. I overcame what was missing by learning to seek out what I needed and finding resources. I also sensed God using other people to provide semblances of things I was missing—nurture and attunement through my foster mom and teachers, emotional and spiritual support through pastors and mentors and friends, encouragement, strength, patience with delayed academic growth, and more. I also began to hear feedback that resonated with me: "You are one of the strongest women I know!" "You are one of the most resilient people I have ever met!"

I learned to begin trusting my inner voice and intuition, increasing my confidence and intuitiveness. I began leaning into my strengths as I expanded my growing edges. I would learn it is okay that I am not like someone else—that comparison did not always reap positive results. Becoming more confident in my own skin, in my identity, and in who God created me to be. Embracing my resilience occurred as an inside-out process of transformation and acceptance. Imagine watching time-lapse photography of a seed planted, seeing it grow as its roots settle more firmly planted into the enriched soil, expanding, and relishing in the sunshine and moisture, until it eventually is ready to bloom and fully blossom with its radiant colors and refreshing scent. This is a metaphor for thriving. Only this time, imagine a seed or two planted for the beginnings of a tree on a hill. Then two trees form—forced to endure fire, earthquake, flood, and drought. The two trees remain standing, with charred bark but green protruding from the branches with new growth—resilience! I witnessed this firsthand on a hike near Etiwanda Falls in Rancho Cucamonga a few years ago. These incredible trees survived unkind and insurmountable circumstances! You know you have embraced resilience when you continue growing and blossoming, no matter the circumstances around you, while still rooted and grounded in who you are!

Moment of reflection

I believe you are much like the two trees on the hills that have endured much hardship, but you are still growing and standing tall. You may not see yet or fully embrace your resilience, but it is already in there. I encourage you to pause and reflect on your life when you chose not to give up, to keep going, or when there was a turning point that gave you hope. Sip your drink, relax your mind and body where you are seated, and take a second just to honor what you have endured, even if it means surviving. You are worth celebrating!

Exploring the idea of how to foster resilience will be discussed in the next and final chapter. Thank you for taking the time to read my story and reflect on yours throughout this journey. We both know it is not for the faint of heart. You are valuable and worthy of connection, respect and love, being seen and heard, and experiencing wholeness and healing. Hope is a tangible piece that is within your reach. All it takes is a willingness to reach out for it, courage to embark on the next chapter, trusting the process, and bravely reaching out for resources to aid you on this journey. You deserve to have an opportunity to thrive. You are not defined by the past, the evil, or missteps; in the present, it is what you do with the now. Life is a gift and so precious. Seize the day. Seize this moment. It will be worth the journey and bring hope and inspiration to those around you that need it. You are not alone. You have more strength than you realize. Thank you for sharing this journey with me. Each day, I remind myself of the lessons I have learned, and the new internal script I say to myself is more encouraging and strengthening words. I remind myself when ghosts of my former self come up that I am not that person or that that voice was someone else speaking over me and is not true. Then I tell myself the truth. Take slow, deep, soul-filling breaths, remember my value, offer myself self-compassion, and remind myself I may need to fill my soul that day with more encouragement. Feeding your body, mind, and soul with good, enriching, life-giving things is what will help sustain you. We are in this together, this journey of life. Remember, you are a valuable, loved, and treasured gift, and your story can be redeemed. There is real hope, and your life has meaning and purpose. God wants to use your story to help others find redemption, peace, and healing, as He has with mine.

CHAPTER 10

My Clinical Work as a Trauma Therapist and Writing on Resilience

But now, this is what the Lord says—He who created you, Jacob, He who formed you, Israel. "Do not fear, for I have redeemed you; I have summoned you by name; you are Mine."
—Isaiah 43:1[43]

My goal in the trauma work I do with individuals and families entails focusing on opportunities where resilience can be identified, celebrated, affirmed, and nurtured. This process looks different for each person, depending on their age, stage, where they are in their understanding of what they have survived, and their process of grief and loss in their life. I feel honored and privileged to come alongside them in their journey. I typically begin with history taking, then move to resources where I learn how each person copes, and then provide other opportunities for growth, including practicing grounding techniques and methods to manage symptoms of anxiety, depression, grief, or trauma. Sometimes with clients, I provide options for processing trauma through eye-movement desensitization and reprocessing (EMDR, Francine Shapiro), mindfulness-based cognitive therapy (MBCT), acceptance and commitment therapy (ACT), brief psychodynamic work, and emotion-focused therapy (EFT).

---

[43] Isaiah 43:1 (New Living Translation).

Many survivors I have worked with have had a caregiver, parent, or significant other and experienced a break in trust, betrayal, feeling manipulated or gaslighted, lack of safety, lack of attunement, and feeling dismissed, invisible, and worthless. Survivors of multiple traumas often need someone who specializes in and cares for the complexity of their story and can sit with the layers of trauma while promoting growth-based treatment to instill hope and healing, one layer at a time. I offer different options and multiple resources, depending on the client's specific needs and preferences, and collaborate with clients on their specific goals, moving at their pace while creating a safe holding environment. Building trust with trauma survivors is a delicate process that requires patience, time, and understanding of the violations they have encountered, as well as self-protective behaviors that have served to help them survive. They are tremendously courageous, brave, and resilient, and I become a mirror for them in that, so they can become reacquainted with themselves or discover aspects of themselves that were not acknowledged due to the lack of support from those around them. This process of growth, self-discovery, and healing is sacred for those who have endured trauma and loss.

I consider the work I do a tremendous privilege and take it very seriously, such that I aim to create safety, grounding, and collaborative efforts toward healing. I learn so much from each individual, and I am frequently seeking ways to expand my education to further provide support to those in need. I have survived and come out on the other side of trauma. I have researched methods and practices, utilized evidenced-based interventions, and have personally experienced the process of therapy and healing, allowing me to offer a whole-person, authentic approach. Often, this may provide some reassurance and relief that "someone understands because they have been there." I feel very strongly that this is one of the reasons for discovering my own resilience and seeing God's redemptive hand in my life: that my purpose is to sit with other survivors and be a beacon of hope to them. Sometimes it is frowned upon for people to share their trauma stories publicly, yet I want to eliminate any stigma that may be present and provide hope for healing. Your story needs to be heard. People need to feel less alone, less isolated, and less like it is their fault for what has happened to them.

In my doctoral studies, I had the opportunity to learn from a few exemplary trauma psychologists, including my dissertation chair, Dr. Samuel Girguis. He was instrumental in shaping my understanding of resilience, so I could further apply this concept in my own life. This experience, in part, is why I created a resilience model through my dissertation research. My model represents a culmination of research literature gathered on resilience prior to 2017. Resilience is a growing field and will continue to be explored. The essential tenets of the resilience model I created combine theories of attachment, growth and development, and cultural theories for caregivers of foster youth and those that work with foster children. It includes providing empathy, attunement, strength-based support, shared experiences, and affirming strategies. The model is as follows:

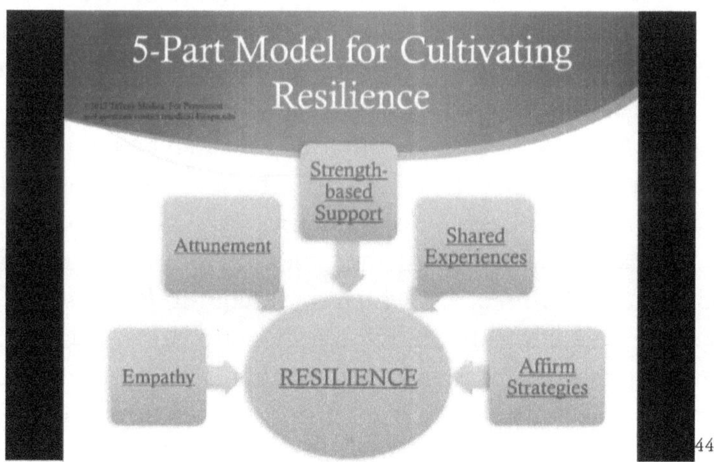

The premise within this model is grounded in Relational Cultural Theory (RCT), which supports underserved populations

---

[44] Tiffany Modica, *Promoting the Cultivation of Resilience Resources for Foster Children During the Transitions in Foster Care and Beyond.* PsyD Diss., Azusa Pacific University, 2018. ProQuest (10831249).

from a cultural perspective.[45] According to RCT, people from cultures that are undervalued benefit from a supportive, contextual understanding that reflects the complex developmental needs of individuals within that culture. The goals of this theory include creating opportunities for connections with others that are mutual in nature and authentic and providing a bridge for healing through relationships despite the violations individuals have encountered. This provides a new, relational healing encounter that shows value to the person and their experiences. This also follows current views on neuroplasticity in the brain, wherein new connections are created.

How is resilience fostered? Through research I completed during my doctoral program, I created a resilience model based on current literature on resilience prior to 2017 (see previous page for a picture of the model).[46] Within the model are embedded features that seem to make the most difference for trauma survivors and provide evidence of resilience, grit, and positive posttraumatic growth in the literature. Consequently, these features contribute to an increase in resilience in foster youth or former foster youth. Note that empathy, attunement, strength-based support, shared experiences, and affirming strategies need to be provided to the individual by someone influential, like a parent, guardian, foster parent, teacher, or mentor with whom the individual feels safe. First, empathy involves seeing into another person's experience, sitting with them in it, and showing emotional care. Attunement, which goes hand-in-hand with empathy, involves matching the individuals' emotions and states to provide support that meets their developmental needs. Strength-based support involves using positive, affirming, and strength-building statements to encourage and affirm an individual. Shared experiences include memories of being with someone and it meant something.

---

[45] Dana Comstock, Tonya Hammer, Julie Strentzsch, Kristi Cannon, Jacqueline Parsons, and Gustavo Salazar II, "Relational-Cultural Theory: A Framework for Bridging Relational, Multicultural, and Social Justice Competencies," *Journal of Counseling & Development,* no. 86 (2008): 279–287.

[46] Tiffany Modica, *Promoting the Cultivation of Resilience Resources for Foster Children During the Transitions in Foster Care and Beyond.* PsyD Diss., Azusa Pacific University, 2018. ProQuest (10831249).

For example, they remembered your favorite ice cream and brought it for you or gave you a hug or card on a hard day. Shared experiences include remembering someone's preferences and what speaks to them. Affirming strategies involve finding specific tools that build up and strengthen or fortify an individual. This may be an ongoing process, as we all need reminders of our courage and attempts to grow. Being seen, heard, held, and valued is at the core of these facets and appears to be prevalent in the current research literature into what helps increase resilience and robustness in individuals.[47]

I have developed an eight-hour workshop to promote training and understanding of this research and the resilience model.[48] Within the workshop, I emphasize the importance for caregivers and those that work in positions with foster youth to identify their own resilience so that they can better help and guide foster youth in shaping their resilience. It is a co-collaborative experience that is essential for the identity development and emotional health of the developing child or adolescent that may have endured multiple traumas, transitions in foster care, and possibly abuse by guardians or caregivers prior to entering foster care. This, in part, is what prompted me to write this book: to share my own life story and describe how I discovered my own resilience so that others may begin intuitively searching their souls for impactful experiences that have shaped and strengthened them.

In summary, my clinical work, my research, and the creation of a resilience model,[49] alongside my personal encounters with surviving trauma, all add value and intuitiveness to the work I do with clients through my innate and experiential understanding of trauma, abuse,

---

[47] Tiffany Modica, *Promoting the Cultivation of Resilience Resources for Foster Children During the Transitions in Foster Care and Beyond.* PsyD Diss., Azusa Pacific University, 2018. ProQuest (10831249).

[48] Tiffany Modica, *Promoting the Cultivation of Resilience Resources for Foster Children During the Transitions in Foster Care and Beyond.* PsyD Diss., Azusa Pacific University, 2018. ProQuest (10831249).

[49] Tiffany Modica, *Promoting the Cultivation of Resilience Resources for Foster Children During the Transitions in Foster Care and Beyond.* PsyD Diss., Azusa Pacific University, 2018. ProQuest (10831249).

grief, and healing. My personal faith journey, a significant protective factor, is a part of my testimony and story that existed prior to my clinical training and remained to inform my interaction with survivors. My hope is that anyone who reads this book may cultivate resilience through growing in self-compassion and self-understanding, compassion and empathy for others, and use these tools as an opportunity to provide encouragement, hope, and meaning to others who need support, acceptance, love, and healing. This is where I pass it on. *May you rise up from the ashes, find purpose and hope in your story, not give up, but press on. Then may you feel moved to share your story of resilience with others, making a difference in the lives of those around you, one starfish at a time.*

CHAPTER 11

Letter to My Children

Dear Jeremy and Rachel,

Your strength, incredibly compassionate hearts, tremendous courage, spontaneous laughter, joy, amazing creativity, and authentic resilience in all you have overcome astounds me! Even at a young age, you have amazing understanding and wisdom. You continue to inspire me and have taught me how to be a better person and embrace who I am through your encouragement. I am so blessed to have you as my children. With everything I have survived, I had no idea if I would be able to have children. Being your mom has been the best gift I could ever have. I take my role in your life seriously, and you mean everything to me. Don't ever forget that. You are number 1, next to God. It is my honor and privilege to be your mom, support you, advocate for you, laugh and smile with you, and enjoy each moment with you. Thanks for being my cheerleaders and enthusiastic supporters.

As I finish this book, there are a few things I want to leave with you so you keep these truths hidden in your heart, and you can pass them on to others. Remember, you are beautiful and handsome and wonderfully made. God intentionally created you for a big purpose and has great plans for you (Jeremiah 29:10–11).[50] As you grow and become adults, remember to trust your intuition, the inner voice

---

[50] Jeremiah 29:10–11 (New International Version).

inside you. Trust when you need to speak up for yourself, set boundaries with others, and create safety. Give grace to yourself always. Protect each other, look out for each other, and for your family. Trust that you are enough. There is always room to grow in areas of your life, but you can grow and still be enough. You can choose who to have in your life, in your inner circle of trust, if they have earned your trust. Know that when people hurt you, it is often related to a wounded part of them. It is not your responsibility to fix them or take care of them. Instead, remember to separate that, hold on to your own identity, and learn to self-reflect if you need to apologize or offer support or empathy to them, and pray for others who are hurting. Always remember that you are worthy of love and belonging, and do not settle for anything less in relationships. Trust that God has your back no matter what and that God has gifted you each with each other. Trust that God is the God of miracles and is always moving and working in ways that create goosebump moments of awe and miracles. Look for these moments when God strings together His golden threads of truth, and celebrate them. He does this just for you because He loves you so much!

Remember that I am always here for you, I believe in you, love celebrating you in your milestones and the in-between. You bring so much joy to my life and a smile to my heart. I have learned to live vicariously through you, with some of the things I did not get to experience in my childhood. I love you always, with my whole heart. Take what you have overcome and are learning, and use it wherever God leads you to spread kindness, joy, and healing. The world needs more amazing people like you in it and to see God's hand in and through you. Your compassionate hearts and humor make the world a better place! Continue making waves of change, and bring joy to people's hearts like you have mine, just by being you. Remember, it's okay to be human and have feelings, to cry or feel emotions. We all have these moments. Don't hold back, silence yourself, or let anyone take your power, but stay empowered, knowing you are valuable, seen, unconditionally loved, accepted, and embraced as my beloved son and daughter and as children of the King. I thank God for the opportunity to be your mom and to know you. Thanks for being the best son and daughter a mom could ever have! Thanks for imprinting on my life.

I love you always,
Mom

ABOUT THE AUTHOR

Tiffany Modica, PsyD, is a licensed mental health counselor (LMHC) in Washington. She is currently pursuing licensure as a psychologist in California. Clinically, Dr. Modica works with survivors of trauma, utilizing trauma-based interventions such as eye-movement desensitization reprocessing (EMDR), mindfulness-based cognitive therapy (MBCT), emotion-focused therapy (EFT), and other grounding or processing techniques that may support clients. Dr. Modica's passion is helping clients grow and overcome life's challenges, providing a strength-based, compassionate, and empowered approach. Her posture in therapy stems from being a fellow trauma survivor, integrating client values and faith, as well as her clinical expertise in trauma, attachment, and resilience. She is also a guest speaker and advocate for survivors. She works out of the Orange County, California, area remotely and in Washington. She is also a board-certified music therapist (MT-BC) and has worked with children with learning disabilities, autism spectrum disorders (ASD), sensory integration issues, and adults with Alzheimer's disease and developmental disabilities. She has taught at Azusa Pacific University in the undergraduate psychology program. In her free time, she sings professionally, plays guitar, volunteers, stays active, travels, and enjoys time with her teens and cats.